The Essentials of Management

PEARSON

At Pearson, we believe in learning – all kinds of learning for all kinds of people. Whether it's at home, in the classroom or in the workplace, learning is the key to improving our life chances.

That's why we're working with leading authors to bring you the latest thinking and the best practices, so you can get better at the things that are important to you. You can learn on the page or on the move, and with content that's always crafted to help you understand quickly and apply what you've learned.

If you want to upgrade your personal skills or accelerate your career, become a more effective leader or more powerful communicator, discover new opportunities or simply find more inspiration, we can help you make progress in your work and life.

Pearson is the world's leading learning company. Our portfolio includes the Financial Times, Penguin, Dorling Kindersley, and our educational business, Pearson International.

Every day our work helps learning flourish, and wherever learning flourishes, so do people.

To learn more please visit us at: **www.pearson.com/uk**

The Essentials of Management

Everything you need to succeed as a new manager

Andrew Leigh

Harlow, England • London • New York • Boston • San Francisco • Toronto • Sydney
Auckland • Singapore • Hong Kong • Tokyo • Seoul • Taipei • New Delhi
Cape Town • São Paulo • Mexico City • Madrid • Amsterdam • Munich • Paris • Milan

PEARSON EDUCATION LIMITED

Edinburgh Gate
Harlow CM20 2JE
Tel: +44 (0)1279 623623
Fax: +44 (0)1279 431059
Website: www.pearsoned.co.uk

First published in Great Britain in 2009 as *The Secrets of Success in Management*
This edition published as *The Essentials of Management*, 2012

Pearson Education is not responsible for the content of third-party internet sites.

ISBN: 978-0-273-75641-5

British Library Cataloguing-in-Publication Data
A catalogue record for this book is available from the British Library

Library of Congress Cataloguing-in-Publication Data
Leigh, Andrew.
    The essentials of management : everything you need to succeed as a new manager
/ Andrew Leigh.
        p. cm
    "First published in Great Britain in 2009 as The Secrets of Success in Management."
    Includes index.
    ISBN 978-0-273-75641-5 (softbound)
    1. Executive ability. 2. Management 3. Success in business. I. Leigh, Andrew.
Secrets of success in management. II. Title.
    HD38.2.L445 2012
    658--dc23
                                        2011050418

10 9 8 7 6 5 4 3 2
16 15 14 13 12

Text design by Sue Lamble
Typeset in 10 pt ITC Giovanni Book by 30
Printed and bound in Great Britain by Henry Ling Ltd, Dorchester, Dorset

Contents

About the author

ANDREW LEIGH is author of over a dozen books on management, many translated around the world. They deal with teams, leadership, presenting, change, communication, decision making and, most recently, charisma (see **www.charisma-effect.com**).

Originally trained as an economist, he has an MA in the field of Human Resources, and is a Chartered Fellow of the Chartered Institute of Personnel and Development.

Andrew started his working career in marketing, later joining *The Observer* newspaper as a business feature writer. His regular newspaper column on Social Services led to a natural move into local government, where he established and managed a large research and development unit in a London local authority. On becoming Assistant Director of Social Work, he led a diverse range of teams, concluding his period in the public sector by setting up and managing a large Adult Service division with over 1000 staff and numerous residential homes and day centres.

With his fellow director Michael Maynard, Andrew founded Maynard Leigh Associates in 1989, now a leading UK development company specialising in helping clients achieve behavioural change at the individual, team and corporate levels. The company's clients include Aviva, Barclaycard, DHL, KPMG, Ernst & Young and Visa.

As a consultant, Andrew advises companies on creating effective people development programmes, particularly ones dealing with cultural change.

Contact him at **www.maynardleigh.co.uk**.

Acknowledgements

Thanks to Abi Eniola, Aiden Leigh, Barbara Thorn, Diedre Galvin, Nick Hine, Nigel Hughes, Terry Holmes for comments and suggestions.

Publisher's acknowledgements

We are grateful to the following for permission to reproduce copyright material:

Figures

Figure on page 16 from *Messages: Building Interpersonal Communication Skills*, 6th edition, Allyn and Bacon (De Vito, Joseph A.) Figure 4.1, page 74 © 2005. Reprinted by permission of Pearson Education, Inc., Upper Saddle River, NJ. Also with the permission of Joseph A. DeVito; Figures on pages 43, 114 and 123 from Maynard Leigh Associates; Figure on page 44 from *Executive Stress: An AMA Study Report*, AMACOM (Kiev, Ari and Kohn, Vera 1979) Figure 1, pages 10–11; Figure on page 66 from White Smoke Software; Figure on page 137 from *Talent Engagement: How to Unlock People's Potential*, Maynard Leigh Associates (2010); Figure on page 143 from *Performance Review: Balancing objectives and content*, Institute for Employment Studies (Strebler, M., Robinson, D. and Bevan, S. 2001) Report 370, February, Institute for Employment Studies (IES); Figures on pages 151, 153 and 154 from *Be a High Performance Coach: A Solutions Guide*, Maynard

Leigh Associates (2005); Figure on page 246 from *Integrity: Are your leaders up to it*, Maynard Leigh Associates (2009) Way Ahead Series, No. 5; Figure on page 252 from GlobeScan (2006), Reproduced with permission of Globescan Incorporated: London, Toronto, San Francisco.

Tables

Table 1.1 from *Emotional Intelligence in Action*, Pfeiffer (Hughes, Marcia, Patterson, L. Bonita and Terrel, James Bradford 2005) Table 2.1, page 40.

In some instances we have been unable to trace the owners of copyright material, and we would appreciate any information that would enable us to do so.

Introduction to first edition

IN MY IMAGINATION, I HAVE a film running through my head. In it, a new or recently appointed manager picks up *The Secrets of Success in Management* and experiences a tingle of excitement on realising, 'Hey! This is really useful stuff!'

The film continues with this person handing on the book to a colleague, urging: 'You have to read this, it's gold dust!' Well, that is my dream anyway. This is certainly meant to be the sort of book I wish I had found when starting as a manager – stuff I could use, as I struggled to switch on other people to do their best, to do what I wanted them to do.

You are on an exciting, creative and rewarding journey, becoming a successful manager. Like anyone embarking on a lengthy trip, it is worth taking some essentials with you. While not exactly a manual of how to manage, consider this book as more like a compass, or a reassuring traveller's kit to support you along the way.

In my most recent incarnation as a manager, running my own company, it's as close as you can get to herding cats. All our consultants are strong-minded, insightful, self-reliant, audience-hungry, occasionally disorganised, successful actors. They use their special skills to assist tough-minded, sceptical business people to examine and alter their behaviour, affect corporate cultures, and rediscover their enthusiasm and ability to make a difference.

Attempting to steer this unique group of knowledge workers towards our own business goals seems at times doomed to failure. Directing them has proved every bit as challenging as managing social workers, staff in a dozen homes for the elderly, or steering a team of several hundred home helps.

The Essentials of Management therefore contains tips, ideas and know-how that nobody usually bothers to share with you when you start out as a manager. Many are obvious, apparently common sense, yet so much of modern management seems devoid of this vital ingredient, swamped by jargon, unnecessary complexity or a straight understanding of the essentials.

One of the most satisfying aspects of being a manager is making a difference, realising that you can indeed make things happen. With experience, you will gradually master the role, uncovering ever more ways to get things done.

with experience, you will gradually master the role

Depending on your background, an early challenge may be making the switch from being a valued professional, where everything depends on personal output and performance, to managing others.

A professional...	A manager...
Keeps people informed	Positions self as a leader
Investigates	Does research
Tells people what to do and sets limits	Demands high performance
Communicates clearly	Acts to make things better
Understands the climate and culture	Understands the politics
Provides reasons	Provides feedback
Has a positive attitude towards the team	Solicits input
Improves performance	Sets challenging goals
Explains	Engages

Understanding the differences between professional versus manager can affect how easily you adjust to the new role.

This book aims to help make sense of your role, by focusing on the key essentials – the core of what being a manager is about.

The tools delusion

'Just give us the tools and we will finish the job,' Winston Churchill once famously demanded, and it is easy to imagine that managing effectively simply means having the right tools to hand. You will certainly never run short of potentially useful ones to help you manage. A detailed 2007 study by Bain & Company identified 100 tools that managers rated as high and used often, such as Client Relations Management, to those they rated as low and hardly used at all, such as Corporate Blogs. Yet it takes more than techniques to traverse the performance maze successfully and make your mark as a manager, which is what this book aims to help you do.

Becoming a manager for the first time will usually be a pivotal career experience and, in the right organisation, will stretch you to the limit. Just to put this in perspective, studies suggest that within the first 18 months of their new appointment, around 40 per cent of starter managers receive a bad review, voluntarily step down from their positions or lose their jobs. As the high turnover of CEOs shows, even the top slot seldom offers a safe haven.

Using this book should enable you to navigate your way through the minefields, quicksand and reefs that lie waiting for the unwary. It may also help if you can find a trustworthy mentor or a coach able to support you in your new challenge.

They need you to succeed

The good news is that you start with a built-in advantage!
Most organisations desperately need their managers on the
front line to succeed, relying on them to sustain quality, service and innovation.

Another advantage you possess is that outstanding managers
– and you can certainly be one of them – produce dispropor-
tionately more value than the average, pedestrian manager. And
anyone consistently adding value will soon prove suitable for
further promotion.

But first, you must survive in this new role.
In most busy managerial jobs, you could probably sit at your desk and do little, since soon
the phone rings, an e-mail pops up, someone
comes in wanting help or there are meetings
to attend, lots of them. Quickly your day fills

*first, you must
survive in this
new role*

with activity you never initiated, giving the illusion you are doing something of value.

What your organisation needs though is for you to be proactive, to rise above the maelstrom of busyness that engulfs people in most organisations and start to make a difference. If all
you desire is a quiet life, this is probably not the best book to
read right now!

Beginner traps

Trap 1 – the allure of power

'If only I could move to the next level I could do so much more,'
is a siren sound you might hear in your head. Many who decide
to try their hand at managing feel this allure of acquiring more

authority and freedom. Yet experienced managers find that each promotion brings its own constraints, creating more, not less, dependency on others.

Trap 2 – 'me' not 'we'

Writing about a famously self-important Mayor of New York, a journalist summed him up in terms of 'Enough about me! Let's talk about you. What do you think of me?' Once you become a manager, it is time to stop using 'me' or 'I' and instead start using a 'we' mentality.

Trap 3 – the DIY temptation

Imagine you are one of those handy people able to fix anything – creaky doors, cracked light switches, worn tap washers. Naturally, the jobs keep coming and if you allow it, you could spend most of your time as a fixer. But sometimes it makes more sense to call in a plumber, or hire someone for a job you can personally do, but which frees you to do something more worthwhile.

Similarly at work, because you know the answers and can get results faster by going it alone, your natural response to meeting deadlines, solving problems, getting results and ensuring quality may be to do-it-yourself.

But this DIY temptation is a trap. Instead, your new role requires you to be willing to call in the equivalent of the plumber, since it will free you to do something more useful, such as thinking, networking or staying in touch with your boss.

Trap 4 – emotional reactions

doubts may start to surface

Think back to when you first learned of your new management job. How did you feel? Elated, daunted, excited, or worried? Most people initially experience some kind of positive emotional reaction at the prospect. But when the dust starts to settle, doubts may start to surface:

◆ **Am I good enough?** 'Can I really do this thing? Do I really
have what it takes?' You are right to wonder about this. If
you do not, then like an actor marching on stage without
a shred of fear, you have probably not fully attuned to the
forthcoming challenge. Be assured your boss feels the same
way, and their boss too. Right to the top self-doubts remain,
no matter how successful the person appears in public.

◆ **Loss of status:** 'Other people will now get the credit for
achievements and build their profile, rather than mine.'
Now you gain status or profile through the success of others
working for you. Their successes become your successes.

◆ **Loss of control:** 'I know how this task or project needs to
be done, so must supervise colleagues closely' or 'I need
to read every e-mail that comes my way'. If you want your
people to feel accountable, you need to get out of the way,
rather than seek control. This does not mean abandoning
your people to their own devices. Instead, show you are
readily available for advice and support. Saying, 'My door
is always open to you,' is not enough, and probably means
the opposite. Instead, show your people you can be readily
contacted, and remain highly visible.

◆ **Loss of friendships:** 'I don't want to lose my good
relationships with former peers.' Anxiety about losing
friendships with former peers, though understandable, can
potentially undermine you. You may try too hard to keep
them happy, encouraging them to believe they can have an
easy ride. The solution is to do what is right, always being
scrupulously fair. Also, let them realise you now act as their
ambassador, making your people your priority.

Three priorities

In the early days of managing, much well-meaning advice may flood in, and it can be hard to define the priorities. Your job description may be full of tasks and responsibilities but, apart from the basics of getting to know your people and what makes them tick, where do you start?

Pursue performance issues

It seldom takes long. Often within weeks or days of becoming a manager, you will probably start to encounter performance issues. Non-delivery, late delivery, the wrong delivery, personality clashes affecting performance, poor work attendance, low motivation, may all rapidly surface as you get to grips with the new role.

What exactly do you do? The temptation can be to hope matters will magically improve. Rather than risk confrontation, unpleasantness or loss of friendship you stay frozen in inaction. Inaction, though, soon turns performance issues into a credibility problem. People start wondering about your own commitment to performance and to being action-minded.

Tackle performance issues when they arise. You may need to tread carefully, but at least start to tread, not stopping until you nudge performance back on track. Once people see you as decisive in this area, the word soon spreads and tackling the next occurrence will be easier.

In your keenness to tackle performance issues though, use the rule of thumb – 'seek first to understand' – before plunging in and assuming someone is falling down on the job. (See also Chapter 10.)

Treat your boss as a friend

So you think your boss is inept, arrogant or just plain lazy? You are not alone. A Gallup Poll in 2007 found that a bad relationship with the boss was the Number 1 reason people gave for leaving their jobs. But if you want to keep moving up the corporate rungs, never treat this person as an enemy. It seldom works as a survival tactic let alone as a route to success.

If you try to stay under the boss's radar, avoid drawing attention to yourself, or keep your head down you may merely create anxiety and that is no way to treat a friend. It is also a sign of strength, not weakness, to ask for advice, support and a clear statement of what the boss expects of you. Assume your boss is on your side and act accordingly. (See also Chapter 9.)

View from the top

Those at the top of their organisation usually develop their own list of what led to success. You will eventually arrive at your own, but here are some of the essentials.

Obtain the best information possible

Once you have this information then trust your instinct and make a decision. When joining the highly regarded US Nordstrom retail company, new recruits receive a book entitled *Rules of the Organisation*. Inside it is blank, except for this:

> Rule #1: Use your good judgment in all situations.
>
> There will be no additional rules.

The organisation pays you to use your judgement, which means taking decisions when you cannot be sure you are right. At Toyota, employees have the freedom to make judgement calls while adhering to a broad set of guidelines, rather than following a strict set of rules. Inexperienced managers often suffer from the paralysis of analysis. This arises from the fruitless search for sufficient information to make judgements fireproof. You will always either have more information than you can handle, or never quite enough!

Really get to know your team

'Put more effort and time into this than you really want to. Talk to them and listen, even when you know what you are hearing is wrong,' argues Dennis Stevenson, the Chairman of Pearson. Alan Leighton, Royal Mail's Chairman puts it equally forcefully:

> 'The first 100 days are key: manage your team, listen to them and remember to get 70 per cent right you have to get 30 per cent wrong.' (*On Leadership*, 2008)

(See also Chapters 2 and 8.)

Build relationships

Most successful managers will tell you how important it is to invest in relationships. As David Ogilvy, founder of Ogilvy & Mather put it: 'No matter how much time you spend thinking about, worrying about, evaluating people, it won't be enough.'

Building relations may hardly seem the essence of management science or a tangible 'how to' technique of management. Yet those at the top have usually spent countless hours on understanding, rewarding and relating closely to people.

Making sense of this book

The Essentials of Management deals with the three basic areas of successful performance as an executive: managing self, managing others and managing the organisation. Within these three groups are the 20 key management processes all successful managers need to master.

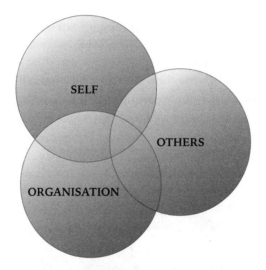

Manage self
- Cultivate emotional intelligence
- Listen actively
- Deliver under pressure
- Communicate with impact
- Network
- Build your personal brand

Manage others
- Show leadership
- Generate team working
- Manage your boss
- Promote engagement
- Coach for results
- Negotiate successfully
- Handle problem people

Manage the organisation
- Manage change
- Make decisions
- Inspire meetings
- Encourage creativity and innovation
- Select and recruit
- Show integrity
- Encourage diversity

This book focuses on people, because it is they who ultimately make organisations succeed, rather than say capital, technology, budgeting or building a business plan. Unfortunately, no individual comes complete with a manual showing how you get the best from them. To manage all three groups – self, others and the organisation – you need to develop your natural insight.

Insight

insight can seem magical if you are on the outside

Can anyone become an insightful manager? Is it something you are born with or can you develop this ability? Insight can seem magical if you are on the outside looking in. But from the inside it is simply based on heightened awareness, which you can certainly systematically develop. Awareness stems from acquiring information, observing and becoming more conscious of self, others and the organisation.

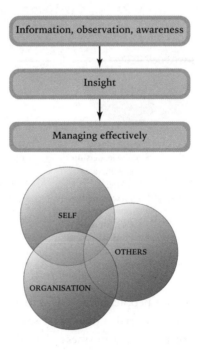

It is a real compliment when people regard you as insightful. They see you as someone with judgement, understanding and foresight.

◆ Managing self, or awareness of self, requires you to stay awake, and apply your insight to how you can grow and develop as a person.

◆ Managing others requires you to become aware of what others need to be effective and applying your insight to helping them perform at their best, unlocking their potential.

◆ Finally, managing the organisation requires you to become aware of the situation, and use your insight to make the impact you want.

Identifying your priorities

Since the purpose of this book is to trigger action, where do you start? You cannot immediately pursue everything set out here. Instead, you may find it more useful to keep returning to pick up new ideas over the coming months, as you encounter new situations. It is, therefore, unnecessary to read every chapter or go through the entire book in sequence. Instead, you can focus on those areas most relevant to your immediate development.

To help you decide on the priorities for your development there is a specially developed online questionnaire that you can use right now. It will analyse which chapters you should read first, and which you can probably leave until later. You will find the tool at: **www.20ways.dpgplc.co.uk.** When you use this diagnostic tool, it will also suggest further reading associated with each of the recommended chapters.

On the website you can also access the entire further reading list for all 20 chapters. The list includes books and articles and the occasional website that you may find useful when following up your reading here. Based on your priority reading I am going to assume you will take some practical action. The choice of action naturally remains entirely up to you.

After using the online questionnaire you will automatically receive a three-month follow-up invitation to assess how you are doing in using the material from the priority chapters. Hopefully this will provide a further incentive to take action.

The best way

'Management is out of date,' complains Gary Hamel, writing about its future. 'Like the combustion engine it's a technology that has largely stopped evolving... .' Yet you have not stopped evolving, you need not be out of date nor ineffective.

No one best way to manage exists, nor would such a holy grail be credible. But there

there are certainly some basic principles for doing the job well

are certainly some basic principles for doing the job well and this book provides them for you to consider and explore. You do not need to feel burdened by hierarchies, overwhelmed by the bureaucracy or disempowered by work pressures. There is nobody insisting you read every e-mail or attend every useless meeting.

To manage well, first decide to manage yourself, taking the responsibility to be proactive. From there you can move on to managing others and then finally figure out how to affect the organisation.

I can't say that I have loved every minute of being a manager, and have experienced some hopeless bosses along the way. Yet, like others who have survived and thrived in this role, I have gained a great deal from it, met some terrific people and, above all, made things happen.

If you want more, it is there for the taking.

Introduction to second edition

WHAT DOES IT MEAN to be a manager in the twenty-first century? Equally important, can you name the absolute basics for being a success? *The Essentials of Management* supplies the answers.

To a surprising degree the role of management remains stable. This is despite cultural differences across many countries. True, changes in technology, work patterns, demography and other factors such as the demand for creativity and innovation, are taking their toll. Yet the challenge remains the same, whether you manage employees in the Maldives, Bhutan, Pakistan, India, Malaysia, or the UK. It is how to get the best from your people.

Managerial jobs are certainly becoming more complicated. Greater automation, for example, means companies need managers able to handle an increasingly sophisticated workforce. Fail to grasp the essentials of engagement and how to achieve behavioural change, for instance, and you are likely to struggle in your role.

The whole idea of management is undergoing a re-orientation. Some even argue it is a dinosaur, since for many it simply implies control. This is entirely at odds with getting the best from people. Years of research into what inspires people to do their best cannot easily be denied. Control does not generate outstanding performance. Instead, autonomy and trusting people to take responsibility work better.

In a much earlier predecessor of this book from 1984 I identified what it took to succeed as a manager. How far has the role changed since then? Some competencies such as handling meetings, presenting, and coaching remain as topical as ever. If you cannot do these well, your chances of long-term success as a manager will be restricted. Other more traditional competencies have given way to more challenging ones – for example, networking, creativity and innovation and emotional intelligence.

Another shift making itself felt globally is a blurring of the distinction between managing and leading. In the previous century greater clarity existed about the task of management as opposed to the role of leadership. Now, though, companies expect their managers to show leadership. This involves them going beyond the traditional tasks of handling resources, delegating, planning and implementing.

Within many companies we find greater awareness of the value of their people. Their unique qualities, their network of relationships both inside and outside the organisation help organisations sustain a competitive advantage. The result is more emphasis on identifying talent and how best to both retain and exploit this treasure.

Try to resist the allure of quick fixes, those seductive 'rules' of how to manage. They sound neat and easy to understand, but they are an illusion. Rules have a nasty habit of being overtaken by reality and sidelined by experience. Being a successful manager is a marathon, not a sprint.

Wherever you work, there is a high probability of sustained pressure to raise your game, to keep doing the job better. This explains why so many far-sighted organisations continue with ever more imaginative ways to develop their managers and leaders. This new edition is a way of investing in you. Use it to master the essentials of what makes an outstanding manager.

PART 1

Manage self

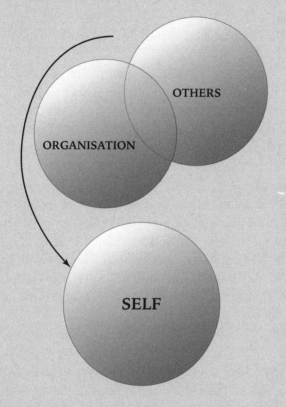

Self

- ◆ Cultivate emotional intelligence
- ◆ Listen actively
- ◆ Deliver under pressure
- ◆ Communicate with impact
- ◆ Network
- ◆ Build your personal brand

Are you good enough? Good enough to manage others and get things done through them? If you are wondering about this you are not alone. Even experienced managers sometimes agonise about whether they are an effective boss and even how to be exceptional. To manage others well starts with being able to manage yourself. How can you expect others reporting to you to be efficient and effective if you are not like that and setting a clear example?

To manage yourself requires you to stay alert to what is happening around you. This implies you are willing to keep seeking answers to questions such as 'How am I doing?' 'Am I a good boss?' 'How could I do this job better?' In essence, you keep applying your insight to how you can grow and develop as a person. This includes all aspects of your life, not just your managerial role.

This first section of *The Essentials of Management* includes six critical areas where managing yourself plays an important part in creating success: Cultivate emotional intelligence, Listen actively, Deliver under pressure, Communicate with Impact, Network, and Build Your Personal Brand. These essentials are the ones most likely to help you survive and thrive in your new role.

Of these, perhaps the most challenging for many people is getting to grips with emotional intelligence (EI). Although managers always needed to demonstrate some of this capability, this has now surfaced as a vital part of doing the job well. Many companies attach considerable importance to ensuring their managers both understand and use emotional intelligence.

Here is a final fact about managing self that is usually pushed out of sight. Most managers soon give up working on themselves. The reasons are many, but since this occurs so often, you possess a sure route to success if you want to take it. By continuing to work on yourself you will leave many of your less persistent colleagues behind.

1

Cultivate emotional intelligence

IN A TEAM MEETING, YOU NOTICE one of the normally articulate members doodling and looking glum. You could immediately call them on it but instead, you wait until after the meeting and gently pull this person aside. Tactfully, without appearing to pry, you ask, 'You seemed unusually quiet in there, and I just wondered if anything is the matter?' That is when you discover your team member's wife has breast cancer. You not only feel sad and show it, you also urge him to take the rest of the week off, to be at home and support his wife during this difficult time.

Fighting back his tears, the team member thanks you profusely and says he will do that, promising first to finish his current assignment today. Finally, you ask whether he wants the other team members to know the situation and whether he will tell them or would like you to do so.

This example of emotional intelligence (EI) in action helps explain why some managers thrive, while others mark time, or fail altogether. To succeed in your new role, you need to grasp the essence of EI, and keep developing your EI throughout your career in management.

you need to grasp the essence of EI

After the major impact of a pilot programme on sales, American Express trained all its financial managers and advisers in EI. PepsiCo found that if divisional leaders exhibited strengths in various EI areas, their divisions easily beat their yearly targets.

When you perceive why someone says something or behaves in a certain way, or realise when feelings in a meeting are running high and act accordingly, you show emotional intelligence. You also show it when, despite feeling angry, rather than exploding or suppressing it, you choose to redirect your anger more productively.

Soft is often the hardest

As its name implies, emotional intelligence is the ability to manage yourself and your emotions and relate to other people's emotions. These so-called 'soft skills' are in fact the hardest to learn – they do not come neatly packaged as a discrete set of techniques. Yet in explaining why people succeed in their job they matter twice as much as conventional IQ (Intelligence quotient) or technical skills. For example, 90 per cent of top performers are high in EI and just 20 per cent of low performers are high in EI.

So how do you make sense of EI, and how can you have your fair share of it?

◆ Grow your self-awareness. Ask yourself: 'At work, can I accurately identify my own emotions and tendencies as they happen?' Becoming more aware of these and how they affect you will build your self-confidence.

◆ Exercise self-discipline. Ask yourself: 'Can I manage my emotions and behaviour so they produce a positive result?'

This means expressing anger appropriately, coping with stress, impulses and moods. Can you, for example, readily switch off and focus on the job in hand, suspending judgement and thinking before acting?

◆ Build your social awareness. Ask yourself: 'When I interact with someone, can I accurately identify their emotions and behaviour?' This means managing the emotions of others, inspiring them and developing your ability to use insight to calm, cajole and handle disagreements.

◆ Strengthen your relationship management. Ask yourself: 'Can I manage the interaction I have with others constructively to produce a positive outcome?' This may involve building networks, rapport, leadership, influence, communications, encouraging teamwork and collaboration.

You can see people using emotional intelligence in various well-known movies. There are also famous star performers in real life who demonstrate different aspects of EI (see Table 1.1).

Of course, traditional abilities still influence success. For example, intellect and cognitive skills, such as big picture thinking and long-term vision remain important. Yet when it comes to explaining excellent performance, EI consistently outclasses them.

Putting it more bluntly, plenty of highly-intelligent, smart people fail when promoted to manager. Through low emotional intelligence, they trip themselves up. For example, they prove insensitive to the feelings of others, cannot control their impatience, handle stress badly – their own and others' – are over- or underassertive, lack political awareness and so on. You can still be successful without much emotional intelligence. You just need luck, such as a booming market, weak competitors and not entirely competent senior managers.

TABLE 1.1 Examples of emotionally intelligent behaviours

Emotional intelligence skill	Star performer	Movie example
Self-regard	Dalai Lama	The Good Girl
Emotional self-awareness	Oprah Winfrey	The Manchurian Candidate
Assertiveness	Dr. Martin Luther King, Jr.	Erin Brockovich
Independence	Mahatma Gandhi	The Matrix, Norma Rae
Self-actualisation	Viktor Frankl	Whale Rider
Empathy	Sherrol Horner Lawrence 'Chick' Patterson	Terms of Endearment
Social responsiblity	George Washington Carver	Remember the Titans
Interpersonal relationship	Jan Eller Phoebe from 'Friends'	Something's Got to Give
Stress tolerance	Rudolph Giuliani	The Negotiator
Impulse control	Anita Hill	To Kill a Mockingbird
Reality testing	Hans Blix	Matchstick Men
Flexibility	Thomas P. 'Tip' O'Neill, Jr.	Lilies of the Field
Problem solving	William Ulry	GI Jane
Optimism	Nelson Mandela	Wizard of Oz
Happiness	Jimmy Carter	Love, Actually

Source: Marcia Hughes, L. Bonita Patterson and James Bradford Terrel (2005) *Emotional Intelligence in Action*, Pfeiffer. Reproduced with permission of John Wiley & Sons, Inc.

If you are smart, you can even hide your lack of emotional intelligence, until things get tough, but then the cracks start to appear. For example, the banking industry is notorious for its poor levels of emotional intelligence and when everyone is making shed loads of money it hardly seems to matter. But once the business environment turns tough the lack of EI shows itself in knee-jerk responses such as demanding a 10 per cent across the board cut in salaries. This merely demoralises everyone and makes matters worse. Contrast this with Toyota when, during the 1997 Asian financial crisis, its Thailand operation weathered four straight years of losses with no job cuts. The order had come down from the company's president Hiroshi Okuda: 'Cut all costs, but don't touch any people.'

the higher you rise in an organisation the more emotional intelligence seems to matter

The higher you rise in an organisation the more emotional intelligence seems to matter. No wonder new or less experienced managers, who are keen to do more than just survive, ask how they can improve their EI.

Developing EI

You can deliberately grow your emotional intelligence, as decades of psychological research, training programmes and other methods show. You can learn to adjust your behaviour, moods and self-image. It is not about altering your entire personality. Rather it involves changing attitudes and habits, and acquiring knowledge and skills. Naturally, this takes time and commitment. Therefore, you need to see it as a medium-term investment, yet with significant rewards.

Not only will EI help you manage yourself, it can enable you to extract outstanding results from others. This kind of personal growth can also help you become a more fulfilled person, allowing you to guide others in developing their own emotional intelligence. As with all personal growth, it starts with your desire and intention to develop. You decide what and how you will change: in other words, who you want to be is entirely up to you.

Various well-established tests for emotional intelligence may help you assess your ability in this area. But you do not need a metric to make progress. Plenty of practical actions can enhance various aspects of your EI.

Ways to grow your EI

Make a commitment

Like a dancer who must learn a new ballet, you need to be willing to throw yourself into personal change, through constant exercise and rehearsal. For instance, what aspects of yourself do you want to retain and possibly enhance? Having a positive attitude towards personal growth explains why people persist and achieve real change.

Obtain feedback

Even the best actors need regular, honest feedback about how they come across. We are all at risk from the boiled frog syndrome in which slow changes occur, without one being entirely aware of them until too late.

Who will tell you the truth? Who, like the Roman emperors riding in triumph will whisper in your ear, 'You are only human.' That is, who might suggest changes in your behaviour? For instance, if you ask, 'Did I do that presentation well or not?' will the response be guarded or deceptively reassuring? Find ways to make it easy for people to give you honest feedback. Constantly seek out those willing to offer frank insight and suggest effective ways to try new forms of behaviour.

Dig down

Explore issues such as your personal values and your core philosophy, even when this seems far removed from the daily maelstrom of life. Work at clarifying what aspects of yourself you want to preserve, keep and relish, and those you would like to change, stimulate to grow, or adapt to your environment and situation.

Often you can do this enjoyably through development opportunities outside the organisational context. This might include external development sessions run by insightful people with no axe to grind when it comes to how you might change or grow. Various psychological tests can also help you determine or make explicit inner aspects of your real self, such as values, philosophy, traits and motives. However, tests only provide information, they are not a substitute for action.

Be inclusive

Make your self-development approach a wide-ranging one. For example, don't just focus on weaknesses such as gaps or deficiencies in your performance but give plenty of attention to your strengths too, and which ones you can enhance further. Incidentally, this is where many training programmes and organisational reviews go awry, since they start from a negative, rather than a positive position.

You may have a natural tendency to want to cut to the chase: 'Tell me where I am going wrong, so I can do something about it.' But this is not how personal growth works. Too much focus on failure or inadequacies not only batters your confidence, it can stop you seeing and valuing your genuine strengths.

Consider coaching

Good coaching can make a real contribution to enhancing your EI. It can provide a fresh perspective on how you come across and offer a reality check on where you can best concentrate your development efforts.

By learning to become a high-performance coach yourself, you will sharpen your self-awareness and build your insight into how others think, feel and act.

Allow yourself to dream

Give yourself permission to reflect on your desired future, not merely your prediction of your most likely future. This can happen through both formal and informal conversations, and even through certain kinds of tests. Maybe your organisation has no tradition of such speculative, imaginative exploration. For instance, groups may discourage such discussion, being instead highly task-focused. In this case, explore outside opportunities to free up your mind to create a mental picture of how you want the future to look. This is always the first step in making a new reality happen.

explore outside opportunities to free up your mind

Build a development plan

Growing your EI, as previously mentioned, takes time and it is easy to lose focus, either by not pursuing key issues or by becoming obsessed with just one, to the exclusion of the rest. Build yourself a personal development plan on which you can work over the next, say, 12 months. This can help prevent overusing a strength, or denying the need to adapt and change.

Set specific goals that excite or motivate you in some way. Make sure these have a coherent direction, not just a single aim. For example, merely saying you will improve your ability to listen actively (see Chapter 2) is not enough. You need to place it within a proper context, such as becoming less solution-minded or helping your people think through what they are doing, and so on.

To sum up, devise your own personal learning agenda. Others may have views on how you should change, but you should only learn what *you* want to learn.

Step beyond your comfort zone

Not everyone feels comfortable working on how to develop themselves if it means doing unusual or strange things. For example, on Maynard Leigh's personal impact courses people may find themselves standing in the spotlight of a real West End stage, explaining what inspires them. Initially participants regard such a prospect with a mixture of fear or even intense dislike. In practice, nearly everyone has a great time and makes important behavioural discoveries as a result.

So long as there seems a real prospect that it will lead to personal growth, be ready to step beyond your comfort zone and welcome such challenges.

Practise

Acting on your development plan and moving towards your personal growth goals require practice. Only through this can you build your confidence and achieve the changes you want.

Practice may include experimenting with different ways of behaving, if necessary in a safe learning environment, such as a development workshop. These allow you to reflect on an issue, for example how to be more empathic, be more assertive or perhaps better understand relationships. Most EI growth stems from continuous learning, not a one-off activity where you tick a box and say, 'Done that, what's next?' For instance, in growing your ability to empathise with people, even if you have some successes, you still need to keep practising and learning.

Accepting that growing EI is a continuous process explains why certain managers become so successful. They continually want to learn what works, to discover more about their personal effectiveness and how best to tap into other people's motivations, needs and emotions. If necessary, seek opportunities to practise EI skills outside the organisational context. To grow your team-building capability, for instance, you may be able to create opportunities to practise these in social and community organisations, such as local clubs or professional associations.

Anticipate setbacks

If growing your EI was easy, everyone would have done it by now. As you pursue the change process, you may hit some brick walls, obstacles that slow or entirely block your progress. Consequently, make an effort to build yourself support mechanisms for these difficult times, when things do not work out as hoped or when your experiments appear unsuccessful. This might consist of adopting a mentor, scheduling discussions with selected colleagues, setting up ongoing coaching or attendance at an external event that can help put things back in perspective.

EI moving to centre stage

Whoever does emotional intelligence best in your organisation will matter a great deal, since it can determine not only individual career success but company success too.

Almost regardless of country, the best-performing managers tend to be those with the highest emotional intelligence. When it comes to the higher levels of leadership, research provides clear evidence that those with high EI scores are more successful.

PepsiCo, L'Oreal, and Johnson & Johnson are three top companies who have found that investing in developing their people's emotional intelligence pays off in numerous ways, including turnover, absenteeism and raising performance.

Emotional intelligence also allows you to understand the emotional impact you have on the organisation. For example, you have the ability to create or destroy moods around you.

Moods matter, particularly in tough times. As a manager you are likely to be closely judged by the sort of mood you create around you. People will take their emotional cues from you and your attitude affects the mood of others in contact with you. Developing your EI is therefore a sound investment you are unlikely to ever regret.

Ways to cultivate your EI

☐ *Label your feelings rather than labelling people or situations*

☐ *Make time to reflect on feelings, using them to identify unmet emotional needs*

☐ *Use your feelings to make decisions, and set and achieve goals*

☐ *Turn anger into productive energy, using it to energise yourself*

☐ *Show empathy, understanding and acceptance of other people's feelings*

☐ *Listen rather than advise, command, judge or lecture others*

☐ *Identify your fears and desires*

☐ *Know your core values and what really matters to you*

☐ *Look for the positive value of negative feelings – in yourself and others*

☐ *Be inclusive and let your approach to self-development be wide-ranging*

☐ *Consider coaching to enhance your EI*

☐ *Be willing to step beyond your comfort zone in how you behave and welcome such challenges*

2

Listen actively

Manager: *Why is Peter moving to another division?*
Colleague: *He's been unhappy for months.*
Manager: *Why did nobody tell me?*
Colleague: *He tried.*

Tough messages sometimes fail to surface until too late. Often poor listening by managers explains why problems and even crises arise, when better listening would have avoided them in the first place.

Be known as a listening manager and you will acquire a definite edge over many colleagues. Managers nearly everywhere declare how much they want to listen, yet commonly do the opposite, and instead talk a lot.

Of course, no one enjoys hearing bad news especially when it affects them. This is hardly confined to just the corporate world. Notoriously, Stalin refused to believe accurate reports of German troops massing at the border, before the 1941 invasion of Russia. He even shot the messenger.

Why is listening so essential to your success as a manager? Certainly your direct reports should listen to *you*, but why should you become an expert listener? The main reason is that in your managerial role you rely on others to sum up situations. Previously, you may have been a technical expert, or specialist, knowing a great deal. Now the job involves relying on other people's information, experience, and assessments of the many situations you face.

> *Facts about listening*
>
> ◆ The average person forgets three-quarters of a talk within two months
>
> ◆ The gap between listening and hearing is mainly because we think much faster than we talk
>
> ◆ Our brains easily handle 800+ words a minute, yet we only speak at around 120 to 150 words a minute
>
> ◆ Words are usually far less important in effective communication than other activities, such as non-verbal behaviour
>
> ◆ Within eight hours we forget between one-third and one-half of whatever we learn.

Active versus passive

The sort of listening you need to master is generally called 'active listening', as opposed to passively absorbing information without much reaction from you. With active listening you are constantly alert to both what is being said and equally important *how* it being said. It is also involves listening for what is *not* being said.

There are plenty of useful signs to confirm that you are doing it well. For example, while you may declare you operate an 'open door policy', do your direct reports really experience that? Check it out with some independent feedback!

The sort of listening you need to master is generally called 'active listening'

Start by assuming that, regardless of your good intentions, you are perhaps less open to unwelcome messages than you think. Whether you know it or not, you may well be sending subtle signs that discourage frank input.

Or check whether when you listen to someone you can repeat what they have said. If you cannot or struggle to get it right then again you are probably not in a state of active listening.

Most managers talk well, but the best ones are also excellent listeners. You have probably met people who seem to listen to what you say, yet show little understanding or responding in an appropriate way. This is the difference between listening and merely hearing.

Good listening is therefore far more than remaining silent. It is a state of high alertness with several stages: receiving, understanding, remembering, evaluating and responding.

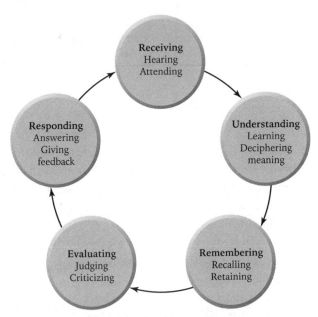

Source: From De Vito, Joseph A. *Messages: Building Interpersonal Communication Skills*, 6/e. Published by Allyn and Bacon, Boston, MA. Copyright © 2005 by Pearson Education. Reprinted by permission of the publisher and the author.

Making it active

Managers who listen actively usually have a definite purpose in mind such as:

◆ Monitor the environment – checking out what is going on and its implications.

◆ Absorb each individual's message – discovering what they think, feel and intend.

◆ Promote communication – attending to issues, making requests, showing understanding, pursuing mission, values and aims.

Monitor the environment

This is strategic listening. You filter out irrelevant messages to build a picture of the situation that may demand immediate action. For example, you might listen to discover:

◆ what customers say about us

◆ which channels customers use to reach us

◆ what our competitors are doing today

◆ the basis of our competitive advantage

◆ the skills or capabilities that make us unique

◆ decisions or problems that affect your own areas of responsibility.

Strategic listening keeps you in touch with current trends and sudden shifts in the organisation's environment. It is like having a radar device, constantly scanning the horizon for what is happening. It encourages you to think about the likely implications, not just for today, but for the future.

To monitor the environment keep focusing on the core issues of 'What is happening?', 'What is going on?', 'Where are events headed?'

Absorb each individual's messages

Colleague:	*'I'm a bit concerned at how this project we agreed on is going.'*
Manager:	*'It's very important you complete it on time.'*
Colleague:	*'I'm hitting some difficulties which I don't really understand.'*
Manager:	*'You're bound to meet obstacles, just keep pushing forward.'*
Colleague:	*'I'm trying, but I don't know how to deal with these issues.'*
Manager:	*'I'm sure you'll find a way through, it just takes persistence.'*
Colleague:	*'Oh, alright then.'*

This colleague feels unheard by their manager. Even though the manager seemed to be listening, the underlying message goes unheard: 'I'm in trouble and I need your help.'

you listen to discover what people think and feel

In this second type of active listening, you stay alert for individual messages that help you produce results through other people. You listen to discover what people think and feel, and detect when and how best to give appropriate feedback. Recognising the value of this kind of active listening, some organisations now train their people to do it better.

Selective listening

Faced with an individual's messages we have a natural tendency to hear what we want to hear. This explains why so many managers, like the one above, and indeed entire companies, may consistently ignore feedback that might otherwise help avoid mistakes.

Selective listening means we may misread the company's environmental impact, fail to stop faulty products or poor service, ignore impending competitor action, and underestimate employee lack of engagement and dissatisfaction.

You can spot the onset of selective listening when people start using anodyne phrases like: *'I am sure you'll find a way through.'*, *'We'll monitor the situation.'*, *'Let's keep an eye on this.'*, *'That's not really how we see it.'* These suggest avoidance and it is unlikely any action will follow.

By listening to absorb an individual's messages you:

◆ discover what is happening and the nature of current problems

◆ learn from them how problems have altered the situation

◆ obtain clues on how to avoid future problems

◆ allow people to express their feelings about their job.

At its most basic, this kind of listening reveals you as an approachable manager and builds trust between you and those who report to you. It also increases the chances that, in turn, people will listen to you.

To absorb individual messages focus on: *'What is not being said?'*, *'Other than the actual words, what else am I hearing?'*, *'What does this person feel right now?'*, *'What are the implications of this person's message?'*

Promote communication

Active listening also promotes communication by making it obvious you are paying attention. When we are intensely interested we tend to do this naturally, but not everyone does it enough. To improve your active listening to promote communication make requests, ask questions, express understanding and use non-verbal signals.

Eye contact

If you ever want to stop a salesperson from droning on, simply stay silent and resist any eye contact. Within about two minutes they will inevitably grind to a halt. Eye contact can stimulate or deter communication but positive eye contact consists of more than merely staring into someone's eyes. Holding eye contact for about 70 to 80 per cent of the time conveys interest and attention; more than this may cause people on the receiving end to feel uncomfortable or threatened.

Hunched over a PC or laptop one can easily forget all about eye contact and wonder why people find us uncommunicative. Similarly, you deter, rather than encourage communication by continually looking away from people, glancing down or over their shoulder in search of something more interesting, or flitting back and forth with your eyes as they speak.

Develop your eye contact awareness and experiment with different approaches. For example, you might hold intense eye contact while talking but show far less when listening. Or use the 'triangle' where you look at someone's eye for about five seconds, look at the other eye for five seconds and then look at the mouth for five seconds, and keep on rotating in this way. This technique, coupled with other listening skills such as nodding, occasional agreement words such as 'yes', 'uh-huh', 'mm', etc., is a great way to keep the talker talking and to show them you are interested in what they are saying.

Body language

Watch any sitcom on TV without the sound, and you soon see how body language conveys strong messages almost effortlessly.

You hardly need the words to explain the humour behind the movements.

Body movement makes a big difference to how people view you as a listener. The body cannot lie and people automatically pick up inner thoughts, feelings and attitudes from almost invisible clues. Even so, you can influence your body language to send a clear message of interest through minor gestures such as leaning towards the other person, nodding, smiling, keeping your arms open rather than folded, all suggesting that you want to hear more and are paying close attention.

Next time you talk to a colleague try staying conscious of your body language and afterwards make a list of the different movements you adopted. How many of them happened entirely spontaneously and how many did you adopt consciously?

Facial expressions

If the eyes are windows to the soul, the face is like a street poster with headlines on it. We learn in childhood to watch people's faces for clues about what they are thinking and instinctively detect gaps between the words and the actual person's meaning or intention. However, we usually give far less attention to our own facial expressions and their effect on other people. You may think you are only frowning slightly, but to those on the receiving end it may be like a red, flashing, warning light. Your smile may be a mere twitch, but to a subordinate it may seem more like a sunburst.

Facial expressions can support or undermine your active listening. Try standing in front of a mirror and convey the following through your face alone: anger, curiosity, disapproval, agreement, confusion, wonder, amusement, approval, interest, satisfaction, impatience, tiredness, dismay, encouragement, praise.

We often underrate the effect our facial expressions have on people and how they affect the appearance of genuine listening. Next time you listen to someone, try monitoring your facial expressions and see if you can detect how they influence the other person.

Use mirroring

mirroring can be a powerful way to encourage communication

Mirroring or reflecting back the body positions of the other person can be a powerful way to encourage communication. For example, if the other person crosses their arms you might do the same. If they place their hands in a steeple shape, you might reflect that back, mirroring their gesture.

Mirroring though needs care and sensitivity, and must not be performed robotically. When you give someone your undivided attention you will tend to do it without thinking.

Rather than mirroring the other person exactly, instead try reflecting back their gestures in your own way, staying in tune with the other person and showing alignment with their gesture.

Verbal signals

Verbal signals further oil the communication wheels and show you are paying attention. These include conversation stimulators such as saying 'mm', 'I see', 'really?' Do you usually remember to give such signals, or do you need to make a special effort to use them?

Nuts and bolts of active listening

While another person talks what do you tend to do? If you keep thinking about what you want to say next, then you are not actively listening. The latter consists of five basic activities you can easily learn and put into practice in your manager's role:

if you keep thinking about what you want to say next, then you are not actively listening

Five ways to actively listen

◆ *Re-statement.* This is the ability to restate or paraphrase a message.

◆ *Summarise.* This is being able to produce a summary of the main issues of a series of important points.

◆ *Responding to non-verbal cues.* This is acknowledging and verbalising the presence and effect of non-verbal messages.

◆ *Responding to feelings.* This is when you acknowledge and verbalise the presence and effect of the feelings expressed.

◆ *Make requests.* This involves asking questions, particularly open-ended ones.

Not every situation you encounter as a manager demands active listening. That is, not all occasions require re-statement, summarising, responding to verbal cures or responding to feelings. Choosing one or more of these methods is part of judging your communication response.

Watch out for the blocks to active listening

1 You disagree with the other person

2 You don't like this person

3 You feel out of your depth

4 You don't want to admit you're wrong

5 You don't want to hear what what's being said

6 You can't understand the person's accent or dialect

7 Impatient listing – you've heard it all before

8 What you hear makes you feel anxious or shocked

9 There's too much noise and interruptions

10 Your emotions are getting in the way

11 You realise you are expected to apologise

12 Your values are under attack

13 You are self-centred and hear only your own voice

14 The news is bad

15 You are expected to make a commitment or get involved

16 You listen selectively – hearing what you want to hear

17 Interrupting.

All these can prevent you really hearing what is being said or its implications

To counteract the above barriers to effective listening you can take various steps to turn yourself into a truly listening manager.

The seven steps to active listening

First, know why you are listening – your purpose. This moves you from simply receiving the sounds, to focusing on the essential question: 'what am I hearing, what is the message being given to me?' Understanding or interpreting the message is a sure way to be an active listener.

first, know why you are listening – your purpose

Second, as you begin listening set a simple goal for yourself. That is, listen with a definite purpose in mind. By deliberately setting yourself a listening goal you are starting to take active listening seriously.

A listening goal also helps you empathise more easily with the other person, because it encourages you check out their feelings in communicating with you.

Goals for your listening might include: enjoyment, understanding, decision making, conflict resolution, problem solving, information gathering, showing caring, offering support and so on.

Your listening goal will also need to reflect the reason the other person is communicating, not just what you want to achieve. For example, if someone is telling you an amusing story, you are both communicating mainly for enjoyment. Your listening goal would be different, though, if they were complaining about a colleague or sharing a serious problem at work.

Third, listen without making judgements. This may require a conscious effort, since your perceptions, prejudices and other experience can be a barrier to open communication in which active listening can flourish. When you listen while being nonjudgemental you give the other person a chance to make their point and for it to be received in an open, receptive way.

Fourth, identify feelings. Amongst managers this tends to be one of the most ignored aspects of being an active listener.

It's partly because so many managers feel uncomfortable dealing with feelings – their own and other people's.

In asking yourself: 'what is this speaker feeling?' you will be giving yourself a huge advantage over others who do not bother with this insightful approach. Be alert to body language, tone of voice, and use empathy to gain a greater understanding of what the person is actually feeling.

Fifth, acknowledge feelings. This lets the other person know they've been heard and makes them more open to hear what you have to say next. Once you sense the way someone is feeling, describe those feelings as you perceive them. For example 'It seems to me that you must be angry about that?' 'I realise how frustrated this must make you feel.'

Next, you paraphrase. Repeat in your own words what the speaker said. This makes sure you have understood it and gives the other person reassurance you have heard and the opportunity to further clarify their message.

Finally, ask open-ended questions. Here you are being a detective, trying to decide what the person wants so you attempt to respond appropriately. Closed-ended questions just give you a 'yes' or 'no' response and usually not enough to go on in arriving at what would be an appropriate response.

open-ended questions prompt people to continue talking

Open-ended questions prompt people to continue talking. You invite the person to expound by offering an opportunity to do more than say yes or no:

◆ How is the pressure on the team increasing?

◆ Can you give me some examples?

◆ What do you think we could do about the situation?

◆ What do you need to do about it?

◆ What happened?

◆ How can I help?

Seven steps to active listening

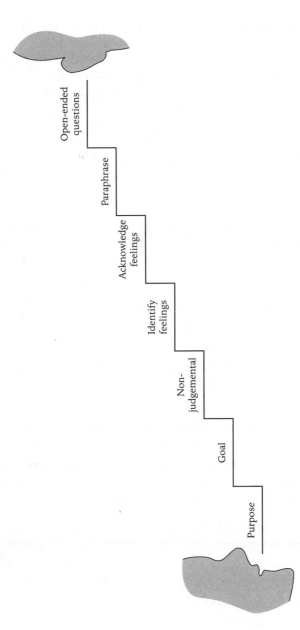

Open-ended questions

Paraphrase

Acknowledge feelings

Identify feelings

Non-judgemental

Goal

Purpose

Avoid being a difficult listener

When you are with other people do you find it relatively easy to stay silent? It is a listening strength to feel comfortable with silence, leaving plenty of airtime for others to communicate. But, your ease with silence could also make you seem passive and a difficult listener. Equally, if you have a lot to say, silence may not exactly be your natural strength.

Difficult listeners are people who behave in ways that make it hard for others to be forthcoming or to feel comfortable with the communication process. For a manager this can be deadly, cutting you off from receiving essential information, such as the build-up to an avoidable crisis, or from learning of problems and what to do about them in time. Here is what difficult listeners do:

◆ Give little or no feedback. This kind of static listener remains almost motionless with few facial expressions.
  Try responding to specific comments with different expressions, for example, smiling, using eye contact creatively, nodding, sitting forward in response to something someone has said.

◆ Offer monotonous feedback. You appear to be listening but your responses hardly vary, regardless of what the other person says.
  Experiment with different ways of offering feedback, for example, asking questions, sharing a story, offering some new information, building on what the person has just said.

◆ Overreact. You give extreme responses to just about everything and your reaction is excessively intense, even when the other person says something low key or neutral.
  Try taking notes or drawing a mind map to distract you from becoming overinvolved while still staying present.

◆ Show avoidance. You nod and offer apparent encouragement while looking around at others, but seldom at the person talking.

Try keeping your attention steadily on the other person when they are speaking and hold it there briefly, even when they stop talking.

◆ Seem preoccupied. While someone is talking or wanting attention you fiddle with papers, look distracted or multitask, perhaps using a laptop or mobile phone.

Try putting all distractions out of reach, including turning off your mobile and retain eye contact.

◆ Interrupt. This is a sure way to show lack of attention. It also conveys disrespect for the other person.

Try counting to 10 after someone has stopped speaking before responding. Also, while listening, give yourself some tasks such as trying to detect what the person might be feeling, or working out how to build on what they have said.

Do you do any of these things? If so, they could undermine you as an effective listener. If you are unsure, ask colleagues to give you feedback on how they experience you as a listener.

Ways to be an active listener

☐ *Focus your listening by adopting a definite purpose*

☐ *Listen strategically – that is, listen for the bigger picture*

☐ *Don't merely listen, show you are paying attention*

☐ *Use and maintain eye contact, without doing it excessively*

☐ *Seek to understand both facts and feelings*

☐ *Empathy builds your relationships with people but make sure it's genuine*

☐ *Reflect back feelings – demonstrate that you have noticed them*

☐ *Use paraphrasing and summarising to convey effective listening*

☐ *Avoid being a difficult listener by offering clear feedback and not interrupting*

3

Deliver under pressure

WHAT DO YOU WANT TO BE REMEMBERED FOR? Presumably, not as that crazy manager who worked absurd hours making everyone else's life a misery? As you try to unwind at home do you want your BlackBerry to decide whether you can? When your children ask you to attend their school concert, don't you want to be in the front row? Will you grudgingly attend local community teacher events and be the one who keeps getting calls and tapping away frenetically on your phone?

Everywhere managers are under pressure. There is widespread expectation of producing more with less. Time seems in ever shorter supply. Meanwhile, information for making sense of the world explodes in all directions. It all amounts to a level of bombardment on managers that can and sometimes does prove overwhelming.

There's a fine line between working flat out and ending up flat out! Sometimes we function brilliantly despite the pressure and at other times everything seem to thwart our every effort. The pressure arises from many sources. Reduced head counts, mergers and acquisitions, global competition. It can feel like being in the Wipe Out Zone. You struggle to beat the clock and other competitors while facing forces apparently designed to knock you off your perch. No wonder well-being and work–life balance keep surfacing as issues for even the most organised of managers.

To deliver under pressure involves mastering four critical elements. Any one of these can create negative experiences affecting your performance: energy, goals, time and stress.

Mastering energy

Are you heading for an energy crisis? UK managers, for example, verge on being workaholics. Most give far more than their contracted hours. Rather than demonstrating efficiency, this culture of excess reveals a weak grasp of the essentials of delivering under pressure. The side effects create low morale, limit exercise time, and reduce scope to develop new skills.

we each have a finite store of physical, emotional, mental and spiritual energy

We each have a finite store of physical, emotional, mental and spiritual energy. Unlike time though, we can re-vitalise each of these. If there is a single secret of delivering under pressure it is being assertive about managing personal energy. This means being willing to say 'no' to wasteful demands on your time and ensuring both you and your direct reports get enough sleep, take regular exercise and look after your health and well-being.

Misuse of precious personal energy arises from:

◆ *Distrusting your own judgement* – leads to doing what you assume others want you to do, rather than following your own priorities. It's a sure way to dissipate energy and squander your time. Instead, keep reviewing: 'how am I using my energy?' and trust your instinct about how best to allocate it.

◆ *Fragmentation of effort* – leads to lack of focus. Countless small tasks may make you appear impressively busy, but studies show it's how managers fritter their time away. Instead, set priorities for distributing your energy and stick to them. People who do this achieve far more than those who don't.

◆ *Using busyness to feel important or valued* – phones ring, mobiles buzz, people demand attention, crises erupt, e-mails and text messages flood in. Your diary is full of endless meetings. It's all reassuring that you count, that the place needs you. Yet such busyness is a form of addiction. What's more, it isn't productive, distracting you from the important things that could make a real difference to your work (or indeed life). Instead, stay alert to what is happening, to the steady undermining of your time and energy. Keep returning to that key question: 'how am I using my energy right now?'

Mastering goals

The awesome atom smasher in Cern, Switzerland is the single, most complex engineering project in human history. While involving thousands of people it retains a clear aim – to make a fundamental breakthrough in physics. Contrast this with the London entertainment venue originally called the Millennium Dome. Aimless, it lay almost derelict for years. Eventually, a new owner arrived with a clear purpose, turning it into the highly profitable and popular O_2.

Unclear goals – knowing what you are supposed to deliver – are a common source of pressure. It may come down to judgement as to whether a particular desired result has really been achieved. Reduce vagueness with the SMART method for setting goals. These are Stretching; Measurable; Acceptable; Recorded; and Time-limited. (There are various interpretations of SMART. For example, sometimes S stands for Specific. But in the version used here it is contained within M for Measurable.)

Stretching

People generally respond to stretching or challenging goals since these put them on their mettle. Since this is well known, there is tendency to insist on over-ambitious goals. These, though, can prove damaging and take years to remedy. Make sure your chosen goals will not just deliver important organisational results but will help you grow and develop as a person.

people generally respond to stretching or challenging goals

Measurable

When Boeing decided to launch the 727 airliner its aim might have been to build 'the best passenger plane in the world'. Thousands and thousands of engineers and designers could not coalesce around such a grandiose vision. Instead, Boeing managers chose the SMART goal of: build a plane to a strict timetable, it must seat 131 passengers, fly non-stop from Miami to New York City, and be able to land at La Guardia's particularly short runway 4-22 of less than a mile.

Trying to make every goal measurable can be like chasing a phantom. Soft areas like the quality of client relationships may only be assessed indirectly, rather than by a single metric. It may even become counterproductive, as happened at Rentokil. The CEO publicly admitted to spending years trying to abandon his much publicised, self-imposed goal of increasing annual earnings by 20 per cent. This unrealistic goal implied that ultimately the entire nation would end up working for the company!

Acceptable

A common problem of delivering under pressure is the nature of the goal itself. It is important that you strike a balance between goals you find acceptable and ones your boss or senior manager regards as suitably challenging. With those people you manage, they tend to choose goals that are more ambitious than the ones set for them. Consequently, you may need to steer colleagues towards goals that, while acceptable, are also achievable. Explain the result you want and allow them time to explore it. Seek a balance between acceptable and tough goals. Think of it as a seesaw, with tough at one end and acceptable at the other.

Make the goal too difficult and people will become disillusioned, unable to give it their wholehearted commitment. Make it too easy and it may not prove challenging enough. Seek a goal that achieves a balance.

Mandatory goals

Like Moses bringing tablets from the mountain, you may sometimes receive goals handed down from senior colleagues you must sell to your people. Non-negotiable goals may win reluctant compliance but gain little commitment. You will first have to inspire people in some way. Begin by explaining why the goal is worth reaching for and why it is non-negotiable. Goals arrived at through negotiation tend to be more effective at switching on people's energy and enthusiasm.

Imposed goals	Negotiated goals
◆ Limit debate	◆ Encourage creativity
◆ Minimise uncertainty	◆ Promote participation
◆ Override conflicts	◆ Gain commitment
◆ Useful in a crisis	◆ Develop trust
◆ Simplify communications	◆ Encourage responsibility
◆ Reflect management priorities	◆ Expand individual influence
◆ Inspiration of challenge	◆ Value people
◆ Reduce personal autonomy	◆ Promote personal autonomy

Recorded

You can probably retain an important goal in your head. It becomes harder tracking several dozen. With several colleagues each striving towards a series of goals, you will find it helpful to document them. One of the best ways is to use visuals, screens or wall charts. Putting goals on display for all to see energises people, but only if they have signed up to them in the first place. Otherwise, they become mere slogans.

Time-limited

Time limits clarify expectations and add a sense of urgency. But only if they cannot easily be ignored. Help your people understand the likely consequence of not delivering on time.

time limits clarify expectations and add a sense of urgency

Avoid target tyranny when the time limit becomes an obsession. Circumstances change, goals themselves may need to alter and time limits may need adjusting.

Goal-setting tips

◆ Express your goals positively. 'Deliver an outstanding presentation' is a more useful goal than 'Don't screw up this presentation.'

◆ Go for precision. Dates, times and amounts help you measure achievement. You will gain the satisfaction of knowing you have achieved the goal.

◆ Prioritise. Several goals can be confusing, rank them by giving each a priority. This can reduce a sense of overwhelm and direct your attention to the most important ones.

◆ Write down goals. This makes them more concrete, giving them more force.

◆ Break large goals into small ones. Making them more achievable gives more opportunities for satisfaction.

◆ Set personal performance goals, not business outcome goals. While the latter may drive personal performance goals, they can be dispiriting if you fail to achieve them for reasons beyond your control. By basing goals on personal performance you retain control over whether you achieve them and gain satisfaction from them.

◆ Make goals realistic. Choose goals you or colleagues can achieve or reasonably reach. Super-ambitious goals can be dispiriting rather than inspiring.

Mastering time

What do you cost per hour? This is a good starting point for tackling colleagues' time issues. Take your present salary figure and double it, to allow for overheads. Divide by the number of hours in the year you work for the organisation. Exclude leisure time such as thinking about work in the bath or reading reports while on holiday.

Your cost per hour can be shocking when you realise how expensive you are! Keep reminding yourself of this hourly rate when deciding how to spend your time. Share with your direct reports what you cost per hour. Ask them to calculate their rates and discuss it with them.

Urgency versus importance

This is a particularly useful way to focus both your time and energy. It can make immediate sense of many difficult choices about how to use your energy.

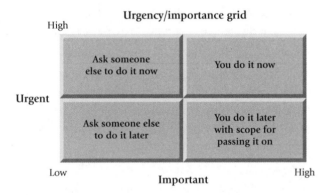

Weighing importance against urgency proves to be a powerful way to decide what action you personally should take. Should you become directly involved or let others have a role? Only when an issue is both urgent and important should you insist on direct involvement. The rest you can usually pass on entirely or partly to others – i.e. delegate.

To do list

Sometimes it's the simplest tools that help handle pressure. Writing down intentions explains the secret of many managers' success in delivering under pressure. Whether you rely on a notepad, hand-held computer, or some other system, keep a list of important tasks and use it daily. The two most useful ways to track activity are the Daily To Do List and The Master List. The former names what you will achieve by the end of the day. Limit this to only 10 items. Any more and you risk ending the day dissatisfied, exhausted or both. For each item ask will it: add value to the company? Be a creative contribution? Help others to be more effective? Help me/us move towards a key target?

Your Master List contains everything you think you must do – sometime. Some people find it useful to categorise this list into different priority groups. Moving uncompleted items from your Daily List to the Master List will rapidly clog it up. Instead, review whether you can get someone else to do the task or whether you can simply abandon the item.

There are numerous online tools that support action lists. For example Vitalist.com, **http://tadalist.com/**, or consider the more eclectic mix of monitoring methods at **http://rememberthemilk.com/**.

Cut the clutter

Work pressures will feel less oppressive if your surroundings emanate calm and order. Clutter includes paperwork, e-mails, voice mails and your work environment. Clutter is like a mental virus. It is nastily invasive and messes with the mind, creating a sense of being disorganised, even if you are not. It also sends a negative message: 'I am overwhelmed'. Some people, though, *like* clutter, mistakenly thinking it says 'look how busy I am'. But in reality it tends to reveal a silent cry for help: 'I am not coping.'

It's neither kind nor understanding to tolerate clutter around you. If people look overwhelmed, say so, and offer help. Clutter is a great conversation starter. Incidentally, clutter can be physical such as piles of folders and paperwork. Equally it can be e-mail inboxes bursting with hundreds of mails, unscheduled phone calls or constant interruptions.

rather than passively answering whenever your phone rings, set specific times for when you will be available, and when not

Frantic phoning

Take back your life. Rather than passively answering whenever your phone rings, set specific times for when you will be available, and when not. Make this clear to people. Impossible? Unrealistic? If it seems that way then your phone is now running your life and not the other way around.

Phone time savers

◆ Rather than making calls randomly, group them into a fixed time slot.

◆ Avoid playing phone tag with those you want to reach. Suggest a time to talk, then be at your desk or free to talk on your mobile.

◆ Never leave a message on answering machines asking the person to call you back. This hands them the initiative, while you sit waiting powerless.

◆ Receiving constant text messages may give the illusion you are in the swim. Few will be critical. Rather than reading them whenever they arrive, check only every few hours.

Fight e-mail addiction

You are working on an important project and up pops a screen note saying you have an e-mail message. What happens next? Even though this can derail you from your current task, you stop what you're doing and open up the message. Most times it turns out to be irrelevant, or of low priority. Some managers go through their entire day like this. No sooner do they become engaged in something important and meaningful when – ching! They stop what they are doing to read a notice about a new e-mail. What makes us do this? It's borderline neurotic behaviour.

Psychologists explain it is part of e-mail addiction (see for example: **http://mindhacks.com/2006/09/19/why-email-is-addictive-and-what-to-do-about-it/**). Persistent checking of mails expecting something worthwhile is *variable interval reinforcement*. Sometimes, a particular check produces a reward. We love an e-mail from a friend, some good news, or even an amusing web link. Occasionally the check does produce a reward, reinforcing the behaviour. But each time you never know whether it will produce the reward. So you end up constantly checking, even if it mostly proves to be pointless.

Google knows e-mails can cause normally effective people to misuse their energy. So it forces its internal e-mail addicts to take a break from the screen by installing an automatic lockout. Other firms help their people with seminars on managing mail and even e-mail-free days.

Try counting how many *significant mails* you receive on average each day. If it's more than about a dozen, act! (See box overleaf.) Remember, e-mails are only one way people can contact you. They can always call and will do if it's urgent.

E-mail tips

◆ Select someone to screen the incoming flood.

◆ Train your team to limit use of the Reply-All button.

◆ Avoid multiple e-mail addresses.

◆ Remove yourself from voluntary distribution lists.

◆ Use only a few e-mail folders.

◆ Do not expect to read all your messages.

◆ Invest in a spam filter and do not open up the mails it collects.

◆ Avoid printing out e-mails, it's expensive and time wasting.

◆ Turn off 'you've got mail' sounds or verbal cues to prevent the tempting distraction of automatic notifications of new messages.

◆ Work on your computer in 'offline' mode. You don't need to be notified when you receive a new e-mail. People can wait. Yes, even your boss.

◆ Let messages accumulate in your inbox and then batch process a whole bunch of messages at once.

◆ Check e-mail only twice a day. Tell people your new policy of checking e-mail at mid-day and last thing at night. If it's truly urgent they can call you.

◆ Don't check e-mail first thing in the morning. This is a tough call, but it will often divert you from getting on with your two most important priorities of the day.

Mastering stress

The symptoms of stress have hardly changed in millennia. Plato's assertion that 'all diseases of the body proceed from the mind or soul' is now reality. Contemporary experts claim the mind is directly responsible for 90 per cent of all illness and disease. Managers commonly neglect their own health and well-being often until too late. For some, the adrenaline rush of the job is so addictive they find it hard to break away. Meanwhile, nearly one-third of employees say their boss ignores workplace stress.

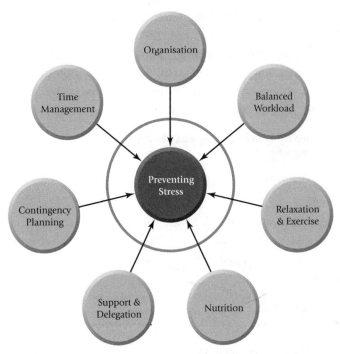

© Copyright Maynard Leigh Associates, used with permission.

How you handle stress will determine whether your managerial career is a short or a long one. The basic message is:

◆ *Awareness* – learn to recognise the signs.

◆ *Management* – take practical action before, not after, the adverse results set in.

◆ *Prevention* – adopt longer-term strategies to handle stress productively.

Stress has a purpose

Many of us actually enjoy working under pressure. Elite performers thrive on it and even deliver brilliantly when the heat is turned up. 'You can't stay at the top if you aren't comfortable in high-stress situations,' claims one well-known sports psychologist and executive coach. Equally, too little stress may cause problems. Behavioural scientists find an important link between it and performance and motivation.

Relationship between stress and job performance

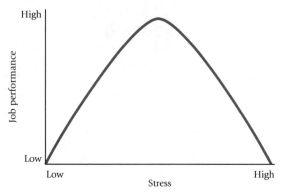

Source: Ari Kiev, M.D., and Vera Kohn. 'Executive Stress,' *An AMA Study Report* (New York: AMACOM, 1979), pp. 10–11.

This inverted U-shaped relationship between stress and performance shows why it pays to approach stress in a thoughtful and informed way. Too little stress and you or your people may perform badly. Too much may produce the same result or worse, undermining health and well-being.

Manage your own stress

To help others with their stress, first master your own. If your initial response to this is: 'I don't suffer from stress', watch out! It could be your unconscious way of avoiding the reality of life at work. Early in life we encounter the challenge of handling stress. For example, we soon realise that to achieve anything or deal with setbacks we must acquire resilience.

This can be vital, including dealing with your own moods. Yours may not be something you take much notice of, yet others surely will. They will tend to take their emotional cues from you, even when you keep a low profile. Your reactions to adversity can influence those around you. Do you get angry, disappointed, ranting and raving at anyone who will listen? Do you go morose and downbeat? Or does adversity become a healthy form of stress bringing out the best in you?

Mastering the pressure from stress involves turning a negative experience, one that potentially generates stress, into a productive one – where you counter adversity with resilience.

Spot the signs

Would you recognise your own stress symptoms (see box below)? There are established norms for when you should obtain help to tackle stress. These apply both to your own job and to those you manage. Absence rates are one of the most revealing signs to monitor. Incidentally, stress is now the second most common cause of absence

there are established norms for when you should obtain help to tackle stress

amongst employees who take an average of 21 days to recover and return to work.

> ## *Signs you are under stress*
>
> ### Physical
>
> Breathless; headaches; fainting spells; chest pains; sweating; nervous twitches; cramps or muscle spasms; pins and needles; high blood pressure; feeling sick or dizzy; constant tiredness; restlessness; sleeping problems; constipation or diarrhoea; craving for food; indigestion or heartburn; lack of appetite; sexual difficulties.
>
> ### Feelings
>
> Aggressive; loss of interest in others; irritable; no interest in life; depressed; neglected; bad or ugly; there's no-one to confide in; fearing diseases; fearing failure; loss of sense of humour; dreading the future.
>
> ### Behaviour
>
> Difficulty making decisions; avoiding difficult situations; frequently crying; difficulty concentrating; nail biting; denying there's a problem; unable to show true feelings.

Be adaptable

According to research, those who live longest tend to be best at adapting to life's changes. Part of being resilient and coping with pressure is a readiness to adapt to changing situations or ones that carry a strong emotional charge. For example, re-organisations, redundancy and cutbacks can all create high levels of stress. Yet, often the actual outcome proves to be less bad, with new opportunities opening up that were previously missing.

Be assertive

Handling pressures demands a certain degree of assertiveness. Being willing to say 'no' in the face of unreasonable demands, for example, can be an important way to counter stress. For managers this can be incredibly challenging – for example, getting across your resistance as reasonable and not obstructive. Downsizing, cutbacks, mergers and re-organisations may all impose fresh expectations. They generate stress by removing your autonomy and sense of being in control. It is important to be assertive and to communicate when you feel the demands being made on you are excessive. Not doing so may merely lead to even more pressures.

Counter-attack

You might think that one of the most stressful jobs in the world is being a racing driver or a steeplejack. In fact, it is being a professional dancer. The daily regime is gruelling. Only by sticking to strict routines, the discipline of lengthy warm-ups, and carefully timed breaks, do the most dedicated dancers avoid injury and minimise the effects of stress. Like a dancer, unless you take control over your body and your life, you cannot expect to handle stress well. Prevention is by far the best strategy. A sure way of handling stress is becoming skilled at prioritising work – see urgency and importance grid above, and if necessary, obtaining help with time and goals.

Reactions to stress vary depending on your personality – see box overleaf.

Who is most vulnerable?

Research identifies two basic personality types, one of which is more susceptible to stress than the other.

Type A is the most stress prone: excessively competitive, impatient, and with a significant sense of urgency and time. Such personalities aim to accomplish too much or become involved in too many activities. To compensate, they put increasing effort into less and less time. For them stress is a constant companion. At the extreme they are people who would rather die than fail.

Type B is free of the habits of Type A: more relaxed, easy going, and not driven by the clock, more patient and feel less hostility. Such personalities can play, relax and have fun without the need to constantly prove they are superior.

An effective route to handling stress is adopting behaviour linked to a Type B personality. This includes:

◆ Allow more time for activities than they seem to require.

◆ Wake up 15 to 20 minutes earlier than usual and spend time doing almost anything not associated with work: taking a walk, reading the paper, or just taking longer to eat breakfast.

◆ Develop the habit of listening to people without interrupting.

◆ Cultivate the habit of smiling at people, even strangers.

◆ Drop consistently annoying acquaintances.

◆ Do not frequent restaurants and theatres where delays can be expected.

- Avoid appointments at definite times if possible.

- Carry a book around and read it when required to wait.

- Verbalise appreciation to workers and others who perform their jobs well.

- Avoid the phrase 'I told you so'.

- Find time each day to be alone.

There are plenty of other ways to tackle stress under your watch. Here are some of them.

Take holidays

Take your holidays and insist your direct reports take theirs! Sounds obvious, but if you asked ten UK workers if they used their full holiday entitlement, six would reply they did not. Many managers feel too pressured to enjoy their allowance. Yet what message does that send to those up and down the line? Monitor holiday leave and reject arguments that colleagues reporting to you are too busy or like their work so much they can't bear to leave it.

Talk about it

It can be tempting to soldier on and assume stress is simply part of the job. Instead, share your problems with colleagues by being willing to talk to them about pressure of work. Members of staff, your spouse, parents or friends may all be able to help you pull through. Never be scared to ask for advice – it happens to all of us. However, be careful not to dump your troubles on those you supervise. They already have enough stress of their own to cope with.

Get physical

Had a good sob recently? While you probably won't want to be seen doing it at work, there is nothing wrong with occasionally feeling tearful and letting go in a safe environment. Crying reduces tension in the body by releasing a natural hormone that makes us feel better.

Your body needs to unwind, which is why so many gyms flourish in locations where people feel under stress. But avoid driving yourself to exhaustion with a punishing schedule of physical activity. Regular exercise in which you get nicely breathless will often be enough. Try using a pedometer and seeing if you can manage 10,000 steps a day.

Relaxation methods can require no more than five to ten minutes, yet make a big difference. Have a stretch, let your shoulders and arms relax into a comfortable position. Try shrugging, wriggling and shaking. They can all help reduce muscle tension. Work systematically to ease the tension in your feet, ankles, calves, knees, thighs, chest, arms and neck. If you are sitting in a chair, or on the floor, allow yourself to feel as if the chair or the floor is supporting your whole weight; feel yourself letting go.

Laugh

Children love to laugh and on average do it around 400 times a day. By comparison, adults hardly laugh at all, only about 17 times a day. How often do you laugh? When you feel stressed, laughter can be impossible. Yet it is such good medicine with benefits ranging from strengthening the immune system to reducing food cravings to increasing one's pain threshold. Laughter produces antibodies and enhances the effectiveness of certain cells. If you are short of laughter look around for ways to get your fair share of it.

Obtain coaching

You may find it useful to use coaching to focus attention on the pressures you are facing. A good coach can help people recognise the different factors that may be arising and steer them towards the practical steps for reducing them to a level where they become positive, rather than a negative. (See Chapter 11: Coach for results.)

Adopt a healthy diet

While you cannot eat yourself out of stress, a healthy diet can directly affect it. For example, eating hurriedly, skipping meals or snacking inappropriately eventually take their toll on bodily appearance and behaviour. The best diet is simply a good variety of foods, making sure you have a balance of protein from meat, fish, nuts or cheese, starch from bread, potatoes, pasta and rice and fibre from cereal and wholemeal bread. Eat plenty of fresh fruit and vegetables, a minimum of five portions a day. Finally, cut down on saturated fat from dairy products, sugary foods and salt. Watch for a tendency to fill your management or team meetings with buns, biscuits and brownies. Try switching to fruit, nuts, raisins and health bars.

Learn the relaxation response

Every human being has the right to relax. But often people do not know how to let go without adopting other stressful activity, such as sky diving, rock climbing or running marathons. There are various, well-tried techniques known to induce relaxation and affect rates of breathing, blood pressure, muscle tension and heart rate. You can learn these and encourage your direct reports to learn them too. Known methods include meditation, Tai Chi, Zen and yoga, autogenic training, progressive relaxation, visualisation and hypnosis. All these can teach you to stay calm and collected when under pressure. Yet they are no quick fix, you must be willing to practise regularly.

Sleep

The busier you become, the more you need to value sleep and ensure you make enough time for it, no matter what the work demands. Insufficient sleep is a sure route to stress and later ill-health. Avoid work-related activity before going to bed, and if you wake in the middle of night for a toilet break, made it an unbreakable rule never to check to see what e-mails have piled up.

To sum up

The experience of managers around the world suggests that work pressures are increasing and demands to do more with less are here to stay. So, mastering energy, time, goals and stress are an essential part of being a successful manager.

If you detect yourself becoming addicted to being busy, to using work to avoid confronting your own work pressures, it is time to answer the final subversive question:

'Why don't I want to go home?'

Ways to deliver under pressure

☐ *Show people you care about stress and be prepared to talk about it*

☐ *Actively look for signs of stress, rather than waiting for the consequences*

☐ *Become skilled at prioritising work and eliminating unnecessary tasks*

☐ *Use your full holidays!*

☐ *Take back control of your schedule and how you tackle problems*

☐ *Share your stress levels with colleagues but avoid dumping them on others*

☐ *Take regular exercise and do not train to exhaustion*

☐ *Explore different ways to create relaxation and use these regularly*

☐ *Laughter is an excellent antidote to stress*

☐ *Consider using coaching to tackle stress, in yourself or those you manage*

☐ *Adopt a healthy diet to reduce some important aspects of stress*

☐ *Calculate your cost per hour; share with colleagues; ask them to calculate theirs*

☐ *Be assertive about managing personal energy; resist non-productive activity*

☐ *Tackle the three causes of energy waste: not relying on your own judgement, fragmentation of effort; using busyness to feel important or valued*

☐ *Use the urgency versus important method for choosing personal priorities*

☐ *Use the SMART goals principle: Stretching, Measurable, Acceptable, Recorded and Time limited*

☐ *Manage your energy not time*

☐ *Take regular breaks to renew your energy*

☐ *Set priorities for how you will distribute your energy and stick to them*

☐ *Resist the siren call to feel indispensable*

☐ *Keep a current to do list with no more than about 10 items per day*

☐ *Cut the clutter: banish anything looking like a pending tray*

☐ *Aim to handle all physical documentation just once*

☐ *Break e-mail addiction by only checking them twice a day. Rationalise your e-mails, for example only seeing items directly addressed to you, not ones where you are merely copied in*

4

Communicate with impact

'PHILIPS DECLARES BANKRUPTCY' screamed the front page. The top team stared in horror. Wily CEO of Phillips Electronics Jan Timmer shocked his senior managers into silence. Belatedly, they realised they were seeing a dummy media story, dated seven months ahead. Nobody mistook his stark message – only drastic cost cutting would avoid ruin. The company subsequently revived its performance within three years. Timmer needed to persuade and influence. Sometimes the only way is to give a severe jolt to people's thinking and attitude.

Vineet Nayar, maverick CEO of the giant HCL group, took a similarly robust stand. When appointed, he found it losing market share and with customers who resisted working with it. Nothing would change, though, until people acknowledged the seriousness of the company's position. He held a series of town hall meetings. At these he held a mirror up to the company in a new way, 'forcing people to see the reality of the situation. Gradually it became impossible for anyone to argue that everything was fine'.

'These meetings had a disruptive effect,' wrote Nayar, describing how he influenced change, 'not because I am a great orator who oozes charisma, but because I presented facts and articulated opinions that had not been aired before.' By 2009 the company had changed its business model, nearly tripled its turnover, doubled its market capitalisation and been ranked India's best employer.

You almost certainly realise the importance of communication. Perhaps you already possess the right skills. Yet, many managers hold an exaggerated opinion of their ability in this area. In particular, senior executives confirm weak communication causes poor productivity. They also warn it wrecks careers.

While the ability to persuade is a vital managerial skill, it has a mixed reputation. It may involve a variety of tactics of questionable merit. These include: telling people what to think; half truths; flattery; swapping favours; loaded language; repetition; manipulating emotions; false comparisons; conditioning; generating fear; and group pressure. Yet, some of these can simply be part of ordinary human activity. For example, insurers deliberately create worry about accidents, illness, or death. Next they offer to sell solutions to reduce anxiety.

To persuade and influence you may need to deliver powerful verbal presentations; and to write with impact. Each depends on judging the situation from the other person's perspective. For example, can you answer that unspoken question from those you want to persuade: 'What's in it for me?' And how well, in fact, do you understand their aims? Do they fully grasp yours, and does a conflict exist between your two positions?

Whether you mainly give verbal presentations or written ones, certain techniques maximise your chance of being persuasive. They include: knowing your audience, re-framing, vivid language, the persuasion pyramid, invite collaboration.

Knowing your audience

Make time to do the necessary research to understand your audience. In essence you need to 'get inside the head of those

make time to do the necessary research to understand your audience

you want to persuade'. This may sound a little spooky, but understanding your audience is one of the first principles of high-impact communication.

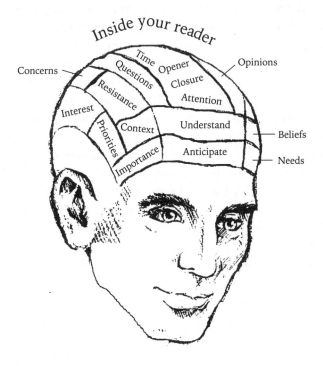

Persuasion works best when you tailor your approach to those you want to influence. This is preferable to a one-size-fits-all approach. For instance, suppose you assume your target listeners are always deep thinkers, ones who like detailed analysis and facts. But, what if one person thrives on scepticism and is suspicious of any new information challenging their worldview? Unless you adjust your approach to reflect their way of thinking, you will struggle to persuade them.

Re-framing

Re-framing alters people's perceptions, making ideas and actions more acceptable to them. Instead of saying for example, 'This report is over long and unclear,' you might re-frame it: 'You've obviously puts lots of work into this, I'm really impressed. It would be even better putting the main arguments early on, highlighting them in some way.'

To re-frame your message convert it into small, manageable chunks that in combination achieve your intention. For example, suppose you encounter resistance to approving your latest project. Re-frame it as 'let's do a feasibility study'; or 'what I suggest is a trial period.' See also The Persuasion Pyramid below.

Your managerial role has built-in power. But this may not be enough to persuade people to do what you want. Ashridge Business School research suggests a manager's authority or credibility influences people more than power itself. Review your present credibility and what might enhance it.

Also, knowing who to influence can be as important as how you actually communicate. To clarify your target audience, try drawing a chart showing the various stakeholders and how they relate to each other. It might, for example, use lines to indicate relationships: solid lines for strong relationships, dotted ones for weak relationships.

Vivid language

To bring their message alive, great persuaders use vivid language. But they seldom rely on this alone, adding in strong evidence. They convert hard-to-recall facts, for example, into spellbinding stories. Dry-as-dust evidence becomes amusing anecdotes. Dull tables morph into moving metaphors, and logical conclusions translate into personal experiences. For example, Steve Jobs of Apple once gave a compelling speech to Stanford University graduates. His message was 'find work you love'. He introduced this rather basic argument with 'just three stories about my own life. No big deal.' (watch at: **http:// philstubbsteaching.wordpress.com/2010/09/13/steve-jobs-message-to-graduates-find-work-you-love/**).

Stories let you deliver strong messages without antagonising your audience or encouraging a fight-back. Relying solely on facts to make your case merely opens the door to argument, debate and criticism. This is fine for an abstract discussion, but may carry little persuasive power.

The Persuasion Pyramid

Try the Persuasion Pyramid to refine your message and make it relevant to your audience.

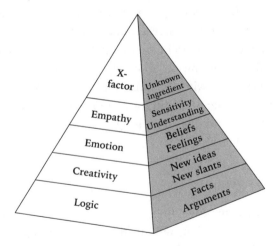

For example, relying solely on facts and logic ignores other powerful ways to persuade. For instance, your message may need to affect people's beliefs and mindset. Or, it may be better to use empathy to recognise people's emotional state. Use the Pyramid to put yourself in their shoes and demonstrate sensitivity and understanding about an issue.

Persuasion killers

THE HARD SELL: Being over exuberant and pushing your ideas and demanding a decision. This hands opponents something to fight against.

RESIST COMPROMISE: You regard compromise as surrender. Yet it's an essential part of persuasion.

RELY ON THE FACTS: You assume great arguments will win the day. But purely factual evidence seldom changes minds. See The Persuasion Pyramid above.

A ONE-SHOT EFFORT: You treat persuasion as single event. In fact it's a process of continuous adjustment in the light of feedback.

NOT HEARING: You ignore people's reaction to your intentions. This can seriously undermine your communication impact since listening plays a key role in being able to persuade.

Invite collaboration

Selling your views to people can be harder than arriving at them in first place. You may often find yourself making a pitch to strangers, attempting to convince senior executives, trying to win agreement from sceptical team colleagues or seeking to persuade people from across the organisation.

Find ways to enrol your audience in the creative process of turning your ideas into reality. Give them a chance to shine. The invitation to collaborate is a 'seduction'. The more space you leave for other people to find their own involvement in what you want to achieve, the stronger will be your ability to persuade.

Verbal presentations

Your heart thumps, your mouth is dry, your hands are sweating. You notice an unpleasant tightness in your chest and a sick feeling in your stomach. No, it is not a heart attack, you are about to give a presentation.

Many people view the prospect of giving stand-up presentations as scarier than snakes, walking on fire, or even death. Even so, few managers succeed without mastering them, becoming adept at giving powerful presentations. Naturally, it helps to love presenting, though not essential. It is more important to find an impactful message you strongly believe in. Your own intention can be the decisive critical factor in whether or not you deliver an effective verbal presentation.

Busy managers face constant demands for presentations. Such requests increase as you advance in seniority. If you can deliver a powerful presentation, it will often have an effect beyond the original performance. Your reputation for being a good communicator will raise your confidence and profile. It can affect related areas such as meetings, convincing colleagues, or demanding a pay rise.

Why give a verbal presentation?

◆ Because of an urgently required decision

◆ It's a specific speaking engagement

◆ You want to communicate in person

◆ Your audience prefers you present

◆ Too many complex ideas to rely solely on writing

◆ Your message does not need a written document

It helps to use a systematic approach for your entire presentation task. One such is the five Ps, preparation, purpose, presence, passion, personality.

Preparation

Can you mentally picture your audience? Maybe even think of an actual person? This is an important step in researching your audience. You could make this even more concrete by having their picture nearby as you prepare.

How does this person think? What do they most want to hear from you? To get inside your audience you need to start thinking like them. Experienced presenters, for instance, will sit in an empty auditorium imagining being in the audience.

Devise the framework

Like erecting a building, your presentation needs a robust framework to support the material. A reliable one designs the material as describing: *situation, complication, resolution*. This turns your presentation into an adventure story. You set the scene by describing the situation, such as a quest. Next you reveal the obstacles – complication. You conclude with the denouement – resolution. Think Indiana Jones, Superman or Harry Potter.

Another sound framework is designing your material into a beginning, middle and an end. These elements make it easy for your audience to follow your presentation arguments.

Try using a visual storyboard to organise your material and bring your presentation to life. Words and pictures can help you arrange it into a logical and attractive flow.

Rehearse

Too busy to rehearse? If so, do not inflict yourself on an audience. Rehearsals are essential, even for the most experienced presenter. The 'quick creative session in the taxi on the way' is a sure way to stumble. Even the most talented actors need to rehearse, so why not you?

Purpose

The death knell for many business presentations comes when the audience does not really understand the purpose. Make sure your message does not provoke the deadly 'so what' response. This will occur when you do not underpin your purpose with a call to action. To give your presenting purpose a sharp focus:

◆ Write down your essential message, or core purpose

◆ Decide the effect you want at different stages during the presentation

◆ Write down exactly the actions you want to happen next.

So many managers fail at presenting because their core purpose remains vague. Either it has too many angles or cannot be summed up easily. If your presentation message fits a short, easy-to-grasp sentence, the audience will usually 'receive it'. For example:

◆ *'Our IT investment can only work with more outsourcing.'*

◆ *'My conference talk will result in new clients making contact.'*

◆ *'We need major energy savings and I suggest ways to do this.'*

◆ *'After meeting me, you'll hire me as your key account manager.'*

◆ *'People will leave inspired and wanting to learn more.'*

Presence

Great verbal presentations rely on creating a relationship with the audience, and for this you must be fully present. Presence is not mysterious magic woven only by the select. It is simply being fully alert in the moment. You are alive, energised and responsive to your surroundings.

It happens when you become attuned to everything happening in the moment. Your heightened awareness makes people more receptive to your message. To become fully present follow the Highway Code of: Stop! Breathe, Look, Listen.

Stop! Before you even open your mouth to speak, you pause, taking stock of the moment. It's exciting, risky yet ultimately rewarding. You are 'arriving', and letting the audience arrive too. Savour the moment.

Breathe. The important role breathing plays in verbal presentations is well known. It is how great performers calm themselves and reinforce their presence. Taking slow, deep breaths before talking can transform how the sound issues from your mouth. It helps you focus and gain a sense of calm and peace.

Look. This part of the Highway Code directs attention towards your surroundings. Looking around carefully you make visual and mental contact with your audience. This may mean picking a few people with whom to make eye contact. As you do so watch for signs the audience is ready to hear you speak.

Listen. As part of the Highway Code you pay particular attention to sounds. Shuffling feet, rustling papers, tapping keyboards indicate the audience is not ready for you. Listen and wait for that unmistakeable silence that says 'go ahead now.' Renowned author and raconteur, Mark Twain, once silently observed his audience for a solid 15 minutes. Without prompting, the audience burst into applause.

Connect

Talking about carbon emissions Jose Barroso delighted an EU conference by almost bursting into song. He quoted an entire verse from the Kinks album, *The Village Green Preservation Society*, to make his point. Powerful presentations connect with people in a visceral way, not only in the mind. True connection makes people tingle, smile, frown, or respond in a way that goes beyond mere appreciation. Great speakers achieve this by stories, vivid metaphors and pacing their speeches.

Audiences hunger for a connection with presenters. Long-running exposure to television and other visual media has made audiences come to expect intimacy. They reject grand gestures and sweeping phrases traditionally associated with public speaking. Instead, they want the sensation of physical closeness – spatial and emotional.

audiences hunger for a connection with presenters

Passion

Audiences want to experience your passion. This can transform an otherwise boring performance into one that moves, persuades, entertains and excites. Passion touches people. If presenting with passion turns you off, think of it as doing it with commitment. Make it pervade your performance, filling it with energy and enthusiasm. By sharing what you truly care about, you will almost certainly seem authentic – the real you.

People anxious to improve their presenting are often uncertain about what moves them. They are out of touch with their passion. The trouble is audiences quickly detect a lack of passion in a speaker. Finding yours is therefore an important part of giving a good performance. To locate your passion, try writing down the answers to these three questions:

◆ 'What really matters to me about my core message?'

◆ 'What excites me about giving this presentation?'

◆ 'When I have finished presenting what do I most want the audience to do next?'

Personality

So, what makes you special, different, interesting, attractive? The answer is what will give your communication exceptional impact. If you are unsure how to use your personality, list your most important qualities as single words. For instance integrity, humour, intelligence, determination, tolerance, inquisitiveness, and reliability. Next ask a few people you trust to describe you, also using single words. How does your list compare with theirs?

Or imagine you are a newspaper reporter writing a profile on you for a feature article. After the interview, what would the profile say, how would it read?

What is it about you as a person that works well? Do people immediately assume you are serious, jokey, in a hurry, or thoughtful? Unravelling this may allow you surprise them by doing the reverse of what they expect. For example, suppose people generally view you as amusing and a bit cheeky. This gives you permission to sometimes be serious and be what people least expect.

The truth about visuals

Few important business meetings seem to escape death by PowerPoint, with bullet points masquerading as visuals. Are your visuals truly visuals? Even when animated or in three colours, neither words nor bullet points are visuals. If you have a slide with four columns of figures and four rows, your so-called 'visual' has 16 different numbers. This is not a visual – it's a disaster.

Visuals work because they take you on a journey. The trouble is: a succession of visuals or animations may simply prove boring and distracting. People do not come to your presentation to watch your pictures, they come to watch you.

Also, take a look at a more exciting alternative to boring old PowerPoint. Visit **www.prezi.com** which provides a more dynamic approach to using visuals in presentation.

Write with impact

Most organisations, particularly those with a global reach, expect their managers to master writing with impact. This is your ability to win attention through well-written reports, concise feedback, or incisive e-mails. Despite changes in technology and pressure for faster responses, writing remains a core management skill. It keeps growing in importance.

At its simplest, writing with impact means avoiding common mistakes. These include missing out words and bad punctuation. The most common of all e-mail writing mistakes, for example, is being so casual it becomes carelessness. It implies not that you are busy, but that you do not care about good presentation.

Typical errors in written presentations

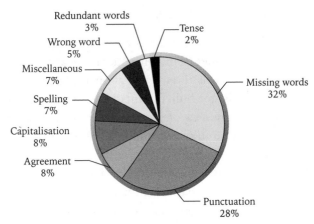

Source: White Smoke Software, reproduced with permission.

The right stuff

Of the many golden guidelines for producing impactful writing, three of the most useful are:

◆ Put important messages at the start, not in the body of the text or at the end.

◆ Use concrete, not abstract words and sentences; complexity forces your reader to unravel your meaning.

◆ Have something new to say and say it briefly; if not don't say it!

Use the unexpected

Reports that repeat tired news, irrelevant information, or stale facts turn readers off. In purely technical writing it may work to laboriously explain the background to an issue. But for management writing this becomes a death wish.

Use the unexpected to hold people's attention. You might pose a question, reveal a gap, identify a problem. You could ask if your readers realise what current competitors are up to, and tell them the answer. You might describe an emerging gap between the agreed plan and what is happening on the ground.

Use the active

It is worth getting to grips with the tricky area of active versus passive writing. Active writing is more direct and often uses fewer words. By putting the subject first, not last, it conveys energy. For example:

Passive: *'The team morale was badly affected by the product recall.'*

Active: *'The product recall badly affected team morale.'*

Or

Passive: *'As a direct consequence of the economic downturn it will be necessary to take action.'*

Active: *'We need to take action over the economic downturn.'*

Develop your style

The requirement for new managers and recent graduates to write with impact can be particularly challenging. Such writing demands both clarity and brevity in which your sentences stay under 15 to 20 words. Longer sentences risk losing your reader.

Also, avoid hard to absorb, lengthy paragraphs. Strong management writing depends on short paragraphs, usually only around four or five lines. The long paragraph can be lethal in the age of text messaging, social media and terse e-mails,

Is your report necessary?

After labouring over a report perhaps for days or weeks, it is finally printed and distributed. To your intense disappointment, you receive no perceptible response. When this occurs you are victim of the unwanted report.

Most managers receive a steady request for written reports. Whether as bound tomes or lengthy e-mail replies, organisations effortlessly absorb information-rich missives. This does not mean they make any difference.

when you are asked to produce a written report first explore what lies behind the request

When you are asked to produce a written report, first explore what lies behind the request. It may be that a verbal report with a one-page summary would be just as acceptable.

Use a strategic context

Whenever possible, place your material within a broad context. Relate it to what the organisation wants to achieve – its strategic intent. For example, frame your report within the organisation's broad aims, plans, aspirations and vision for its future. At your particular management level, you may be unaware of either the strategic context or the nature of existing plans. Well, now is the time to find out. Asking the questions will tend to raise your personal profile.

Organisational reports are not essays but action-focused. No matter how complicated an issue, it can usually be confined to one or two pages. Your written reports need to cover the three simple stages of impactful writing: Prepare, Produce, Persist.

Prepare – Identify issues, clarify terms of reference, gather the information and do the analysis. You also need enough time to prepare. Be willing to negotiate around deadlines and the degree of urgency.

Produce – Structure your report into a logical framework which your readers can easily follow. Provide an action focus with an emphasis on quickly conveying the key points in an easy to follow sequence.

How to avoid writer's block

If writing a report fills you with dread do not despair! You are certainly not alone. Committing your ideas, suggestions, and conclusions to the written word can seem dangerous, even career threatening. Instead of worrying whether your writing works, allow yourself to brainstorm, splurging out as much as you can on paper or screen. Waste no time on grammar, logic, or even the full content:

> *Don't get it right, get it written…then get it right*

The real writing work begins when you re-order the mass of material. Ruthlessly edit for clarity and brevity, fill gaps, and make suggestions for action.

Happy headings

Snappy headings ensnare your reader and ideally sum up your message at that point. You are not writing for an academic journal but to achieve action. Headings force you to think about what you are saying. Readers appreciate these signposts.

Summarise

A good summary is a gift to your reader, saving lots of re-reading. If you cannot manage it with a few short paragraphs it is over-long or complicated.

Persist – This is the final stage, and usually the most neglected. Never willingly deliver your report to your audience without knowing what should happen next and negotiating the next steps. Consider using the three-thirds guideline for impactful writing, one-third spent on each of these three tasks: research and prepare, write, follow up.

The actual writing is usually the easy part. Presenting it and ensuring follow-through action can be more challenging. Solid follow-through involves chasing to have your output appear on suitable agendas and achieve quality time for consideration.

Writing a management report can prove so demanding, follow-through energy may be in short supply. But no management report is truly effective without persistent follow-through. Reserve enough energy to persist with the final stage. Arrange meetings to discuss it and demand action. Invite feedback on what happened since you delivered it. Ask questions about what action needs to occur next and so on. You may even find it useful to issue a short follow-up report. Persistent follow-through builds your reputation for thoroughness.

Ways to persuade and influence

☐ *See it from their perspective*

☐ *Know your audience*

☐ *Use re-framing to present your arguments differently in a
new context*

☐ *To influence use personal authority rather than relying on power*

☐ *Use vivid language and compelling evidence*

☐ *Invite collaboration*

☐ *Connect emotionally*

☐ *Use the Persuasion Pyramid to develop a flexible persuasion
strategy*

☐ *Be alert for non-persuaders, such as the hard sell*

Ways to give powerful presentions

☐ *Use the 5 Ps: Preparation, Purpose, Presence, Passion, Personality*

☐ *Research your audience, even when you think you know them
already*

☐ *Rehearse enough so you can manage without detailed notes*

☐ *Reduce the purpose of your presenting to a single headline
statement*

☐ *Express the purpose of the presentation in terms of action*

☐ *Use the Highway Code of presenting: Stop! Breathe, Look, Listen*

☐ *Connect with your audience with stories, visuals and other means*

☐ *Audiences expect to experience your passion – show them!*

☐ *Use your whole personality, people want the real you in action*

☐ *Avoid death by PowerPoint: it's you they want to see, not bullet points!*

Ways to write with impact

☐ *Explore what seems to lie behind the request for a written report*

☐ *Pay close attention to how people will receive your written messages*

☐ *Don't get it right, get it written, then get it right*

☐ *Make your written communications add value, not merely distribute information*

☐ *Place your most important message at the start*

☐ *Stick to concrete rather than abstract words and sentences*

☐ *Use active rather than passive forms of sentence construction*

☐ *Provide a strategic context for your reports*

☐ *Written reports usually need three simple stages: prepare, produce, persist*

☐ *Use a strong heading to grab attention and summarise your message*

☐ *Provide an easy-to-read summary*

☐ *Make each report recipient feel special by how you distribute it*

☐ *Reserve enough energy after writing, to ensure you can follow through*

☐ *Be action focused, offering ways forward and solutions*

5

Network

HOW DID BILL GATES GET SO LUCKY? Why did his obscure start-up company receive a surprise, life-changing phone call from Big Blue? The largest computer firm on the planet rang because of his mum. As a tireless networker she was friends with the man who ran IBM. Describing her son's new venture to the powerful CEO caused the historic and much-written-about phone call.

Schmoozing, though, did not connect Mary Gates to IBM's Akers. She worked alongside him on the same non-profit board, which helped create mutual trust, an exchange of private information and access to each other's diverse skills. Akers' view consequently expanded about who might help supply a new operating system.

If you are into social networking you already know its pros and cons. But this kind of networking remains fairly superficial and based on weak ties – how else could you acquire hundreds, even thousands of 'friends'? We are under siege from these kinds of connections. Facebook currently claims more than 750 million users, LinkedIn 100 million, and Twitter handles 1 billion tweets a week.

True networking though requires spending quality time with people. Reject any thought that full networking is somehow glory-seeking, sleazy, political or bad for your image. Management is about getting things done through others, and this is where networks come in. They offer many gains including access to power and how to turn ideas into breakthroughs.

Fear of networking

Successful managers tend to be enthusiastic networkers, building theirs into a normal way of doing business. Others, though, hate the chore, seeing the task as an unpleasant necessity, a dreaded developmental challenge. Viewing networking in such a negative way could be a fatal career mistake. INSEAD Professor of Organisational Behaviour, Herminia Ibarra, argues: 'What you know is who you know. Managers who neglect to build their networks risk failing, or remaining stuck in middle management' (see 'Networking is Vital for Successful Managers', **http://knowledge. insead.edu/contents/Ibarra.cfm**).

> *successful managers tend to be enthusiastic networkers, building theirs into a normal way of doing business*

So why do so many managers fear or at least resist networking? One reason is retaining valuable contacts demands constant attention. 'A lot of people who are not very good at this may feel initially they are wasting their time,' says Professor Ibarra. 'They've gone to that conference, to those meetings, to this networking event, and what do they have to show for it? They have less scope to do the bread and butter day job. However, over the longer term or even over the mid-term, those are the contacts that really take off.'

Take Nick Hine, a Founding Partner in a leading UK law firm. He regularly feeds his numerous connections endless information, leads and opportunities for meeting new contacts. At the many events he hosts each year you encounter a diverse mix of expertise. When he passes your name to his quality contacts he expects nothing in return, apart from a thank you note. Whatever your problem, Nick can usually point you towards a person with specialist knowledge.

Know your networks

Not all networks are equal. Some, like the social ones merely provide casual connections. Others focus on operational matters and a few are strategic – the ones that make you think. Operational networks tend to be easy to establish. They involve working with the colleagues who you need to do your job well. This might include an HR person, a customer, a supplier or a team member. If you work 60–80 hours as week as many managers do, your personal network may be harder to fashion than a purely operational one. This kind of network lets you interact with a diverse set of like-minded professionals. This is the one you probably turn to when thinking of changing jobs or career and the contacts usually go wider than your immediate job.

A strategic network can be tricky to establish and demanding to nurture. Yet this kind is essential for becoming a business leader, because the contacts make you look beyond your industry. Such a network allows you to share ideas on best practice and to see the bigger picture. Strategic networks also encourage you to craft your own visionary approach.

Build an effective network

The first and most important principle behind an effective managerial network is: size does not matter. In social networking the emphasis tends to be on expanding almost indefinitely the number of 'friends' or contacts. In contrast, an effective network for your management role is not about quantity. Instead, contact quality matters more. For example, most effective core networks range from 12 to 18 people. Individuals who simply know a lot of people are less likely to achieve exceptional performance, because they are spread too thinly. Also, structure counts more than scale. For instance, core connections will bridge smaller, more diverse kinds of groups. Useful links will cross boundaries of status, function or geography.

The second principle is to build strong ties with those who can offer you new information and expertise. That should include people from anywhere, inside or outside the organisation. Aim to build links to those who can provide mentoring, sense making, political support and resources.

The third principle is to connect with those willing to offer you developmental feedback and personal support. These are people who challenge your decisions, and push for them to be better. Strong relationships like these create strong networks from which you gain influence, broaden your expertise and learn new skills. Restrict membership to energisers, people who make things happen. Like planting seeds in the garden, you can only grow these contacts slowly. Building a better network involves four essentials:

◆ *Diagnose* – dissect the network and what each member contributes

◆ *Restrict* – dump time-wasters and energy sapping contacts

◆ *Expand* – find the right energisers who can help achieve your goals

◆ *Leverage* – keep your contacts involved and use them creatively.

relationships lie at the heart of full networking and there are few short cuts

Relationships lie at the heart of full networking and there are few short cuts. To know another person takes time. No amount of e-mailing or Facebook 'poking' can substitute for spending an extended period with them. Only time and effort allow you learn each other's strengths and weaknesses, quirks, dreams and vulnerabilities. While you can make quick contacts, lasting ones take longer, more effort and have their own rhythm.

A useful way to diagnose your network is to map on a chart or spreadsheet the actual membership. Experts suggest you start by listing each contact. Against each show: first, who introduced you to the contact, and second, who introduced you to this person. If you initiated introductions to key contacts more than 65 per cent of the time, your network is too inbred. There is not enough diversity in terms of experience, training, worldview and so on. Another reason why a network loses valuable diversity is because of a natural tendency to stick to people you spend most time with, such as colleagues in your department.

To restrict a network to useful connections ask: will this person:

◆ Provide me with personal support? That is, help me get back on track when I'm under pressure?

◆ Add a sense of purpose or worth? Will they validate my work by using a broader context, giving meaning to what I do?

◆ Promote work/life balance. Would they be concerned with my physical health, or spiritual well-being?

To expand a network, encourage diversity by using the 'shared activity principle'. This brings in people you do things with, but not always at work – for example, sports teams, community service and other non-work activity. Also, some shared activities are more potent than others, such as those evoking passion and where there is much at stake.

To leverage a network is to make it work hard for you. Leveraging ensures you do not rely on a passive collection of names recorded on a listing system. Start by identifying those who act as brokers, introducing you to people outside your normal daily contacts. Expand these kinds of connections, because they enlarge your horizon and stimulate you to develop new relevant links.

Get a strategy

Devise a proper plan for building networks. List the practical actions needed such as:

◆ Draw a network map of all contacts.

◆ In any major task you undertake review who might assist you.

◆ Keep notes on any potential key contact; start by identifying how mutual help might work.

◆ Make relationship building a managerial priority; devote meaningful time to pursuing this.

◆ Break major projects into tasks only you can do, or where others' help would be more appropriate.

Be an effective networker

Apart from using the above principles to build your network, you will be effective at networking if you:

◆ **Get organised** by managing contact information and avoid wasted follow-up effort. Keep updating and refining your contacts – 'weeding your garden', so the strongest plants keep growing. Consider adopting technological fixes for tracking contacts and regularly reminding you of their existence. These range from the little black book, MS Office, relational databases and networking sites. For example, what happens to the business cards you acquire? Do you file them for quick access or stuff them away hoping they will be useful one day? New contacts fade fast without early reinforcement. This is the job of a reliable follow-up system that reminds you to send notes, letters, e-mails and other support.

◆ **Use due diligence** to improve your chances of making each contact a success. Do your homework by fact finding on those you expect to meet. Rather than leaving it to chance, investigate sources of personal information like LinkedIn, Facebook and allied sites. If you expect to encounter particular people, explore their business sectors in readiness for discussing these. Preparation shows your interest in them and confirms your serious intent.

◆ **Prioritise** because networking eats up managerial time. Decide which relationships will work and which don't. Time is short and you want the best return on your investment. As ace networker Nick Hine above explains: 'You need to grade who you meet, and drop time wasters. Concentrate on those with whom you can develop a meaningful relationship.'

◆ **Listen well** and discover the person's desires, hopes, and dreams. You cannot do this by always speaking about your concerns or relying entirely on e-mails. Spend quality time with the person and be sure to leave out 'me' and 'I' from the conversation; concentrate on 'you' and 'yours'. See also Chapter 2.

◆ **Prove trustworthy** and act in an ethical way. You build trust with others by being reliable, authentic, willing to admit mistakes and confronting wrong actions in others. In your networking make it a habit to always deliver on what you said you would do and straightaway. Embrace the formula of under-promise and over-deliver. See also Chapter 19: Show integrity.

◆ **Value diversity** by recognising individuals have different styles, tastes and preferences. Even when you disagree on minor items show respect for the other person; maintain a close, healthy relationship by basing it on compatible values.

◆ **Offer care** by showing your interest in your contacts' achievements, problems and life. Use empathy to put yourself in their shoes. Do the unexpected. For example, call them when they least expect and demonstrate that what happens to them matters to you.

◆ **Ask for help** with difficult goals or tasks. To be a loner is the opposite of networking. Drawing on a wide range of talents helps you perform at your best. Being willing to say 'I don't know' is a strength, not a weakness.

◆ **Persist** with your relationship building, despite obstacles of time and place. Be tenacious in developing network contacts and use multiple channels to reinforce your aims.

◆ **Give feedback** on how you have used people's suggestions, introductions, offers of help or supply of material. You improve the quality and depth of the relationship when you recognise that people are curious and want to know what you are doing and why.

Be people-minded

E-mails, text messages, or comments on social sites can oil the wheels of networking. What matters most, though, is live inter-actions between human beings. Next best might be a prolonged Skype-type conversation. Two common networking worries many managers struggle with are: how can I feel comfortable in social situations and how do I work a room, circulate and make new contacts?

Live interactions build networks. What does this mean in practice? For example, be willing to introduce yourself by being direct, open and welcoming. Respond when people make overtures, such as asking for information. Don't make the other person struggle to learn who you are and your values.

live interactions build networks

Use the simple principle on these live occasions of always greeting someone with a warm smile and a firm handshake. Use good eye contact right away. Though obvious, this is often neglected in the tension and fraught moments of first meeting. Take the initiative in discussions; ask new acquaintances to describe their life and what concerns them.

Working the room

You are not alone if you find such situations stressful. You see groups of people busily engaged in conversation and it is easy to conclude they do not need you. Unless you know someone in the group, how do you break into the circle without causing offence? This can be challenging for even experienced networkers. The secret lies in careful observation and using some basic techniques for entering a conversation.

Start by getting comfortable standing on your own. Rather than rushing to join an existing set of people without a real purpose, spend time looking around. Take some deep breaths. Focus on what is happening around you, not what is happening inside you. A useful technique is the Sherlock Holmes game. While absorbing your surroundings, look for clues about each group. What is the body language of each group telling you? How intense is the conversation? Is there much eye contact? Is there laughter or does everyone look deadly serious? By the time you have played this game for a few minutes you will already feel more confident about which group to enter and how.

Having selected the gathering you want to join, get closer but remain out of their immediate vision. Wait at a distance and watch for the intensity of conversation to alter. Then walk into or close up to the gathering. Listen intently to whoever is speaking. Do not try to change the tone, pace or steal the focus away from anybody else.

Once the talk changes, explain who you are. Now is the time to speak up if you have something worth saying. Should you have an interest in one particular person say so – for example 'I've been keen to get together for ages, but can see you're busy right now. Let me give you my business card, and perhaps give me yours and I'll call you next week for a quick chat.'

Watch a skilled networker and it can seem there is nothing significant happening. Yet others keep talking to them. They move around with ease, and seldom become trapped in fruitless exchanges. Successful networkers are generally excellent observers and listeners. They are comfortable giving out, and always curious. At the heart of this involvement lies alertness. They are constantly watching and ready to move on without rushing.

Skilled networkers rely on the fact we are all linked by a chain of acquaintances. Scientists argue that in a world of 6.6 billion we are each just six introductions away from any other person on the planet. Called 'Six Degrees of Separation', this holds for almost any contact you might want to make. Networks are the ultimate six-degrees tool.

Ways to network

☐ *Make networking a constant part of your daily life, not a sporadic effort*

☐ *Ensure you build in plenty of give, not just take*

- [ ] *Think of your networks as a series of virtual teams to which you belong*

- [ ] *Study your networks – diagnose, restrict, expand and leverage*

- [ ] *Create a formal strategy for building networks*

- [ ] *Develop the tools and skills to nurture relationships*

- [ ] *Identify the information brokers in your network*

- [ ] *In building networks, go for quality not size*

- [ ] *Make sure networks are diverse and cross many boundaries*

- [ ] *Use due diligence about each possible addition*

- [ ] *Restrict membership to energisers who can deliver what you need*

- [ ] *To make a network more useful, use the 'shared activity' principle*

- [ ] *Demonstrate reliability to network contacts*

- [ ] *Recognise people can have different styles, tastes and preferences*

- [ ] *Show interest in people's achievements, their problems and their life*

- [ ] *Master the two key challenges of becoming at ease in social situations, and how to work a room*

- [ ] *Use network contacts to help you with difficult goals or tasks*

- [ ] *When meeting new people be direct, open and welcoming; be ready to explain who you are, and your values*

- [ ] *Give feedback to your contacts on the help they gave and to build the quality and depth of the relationship*

- [ ] *Note the favours others do for you and show your appreciation*

- [ ] *Be selective in your use of social sites and use them for creating groups and sharing technical information*

6

Build your personal brand

YOUR PERSONAL BRAND is about making you future proof. Or as management guru Tom Peters put it more than a decade ago: 'In the age of the individual, you have to be your own brand. It's time for me – and you – to take a lesson from the big brands, a lesson that's true for anyone who's interested in what it takes to stand out and prosper in the new world of work.' This approach is now mainstream.

Once, managers relied on working hard on the reasonable assumption of being eventually recognised and rewarded. In the worst-case scenario, it meant waiting to fill the shoes of someone who had conveniently moved on or out. Now, though, with flattening hierarchies, matrix-style management and other changes, it is disturbingly easy to remain invisible within an organisation. Without a strong brand, no matter how hard you work, nothing may alter unless you actively promote your profile.

'Your brand is what people say about you when you're not in the room,' claimed Jeff Bezos, founder of Amazon. A personal brand is more than a name, or a description of who you are. When people come into contact with you, a personal brand allows them to form an opinion about you more easily.

The nature of work is changing. The classic job of middle manager could be on its way out. Technology, virtual and self-managed teams, better information and how we interact with customers continue altering what it means to manage in the twenty-first century. Given this scenario, polishing your personal brand makes sense for survival, let alone improving your chances of success.

Strong personal brands

◆ Acting: Nicole Kidman, Meryl Streep, George Clooney

◆ Architecture: Zaha Hadid, Norman Foster, Frank Gehry, Richard Rogers

◆ Business: Richard Branson, Steve Jobs, Michael O'Leary

◆ Inventors: James Dyson, Tim Berners-Lee

◆ Chefs: Nigella Lawson, Gordon Ramsay, Jamie Oliver

◆ Finance: Warren Buffett, George Soros

◆ Motor racing: Bernie Ecclestone, Lewis Hamilton, Michael Schumacher

◆ Artists: Lucien Freud, David Hockney, Tracey Emin, Banksy, Gerhard Richter

◆ Sculpture: Anish Kapoor, Antony Gormley, Damien Hirst

◆ Sport: Roger Federer, David Beckham, Serena Williams

◆ Photography: Don McCullin, Annie Leibovitz

◆ Film making: Ridley Scott, Steven Spielberg, James Cameron, Pedro Almodóvar

◆ Thinkers: Richard Dawkins, Noam Chomsky

◆ Music: David Bowie, Elton John, Paul McCartney, John Williams, Philip Glass

You already have a personal brand and your only choice is whether it is positive, negative or neutral. Most managers must hone their profile to ensure visibility, not necessarily to be a household name. It is usually enough to be well known among one's peers, potential customers, clients, and suppliers. While honest hard work will always stand the test of time, this may not be enough to ensure you stand out from the crowd.

you already have a personal brand and your only choice is whether it is positive, negative or neutral

Personal visibility, for instance, will almost certainly play an important part in choosing the next manager for an important assignment or dishing out the next valuable promotion. Whether someone unexpectedly contacts you about a great job opportunity may stem from personal branding. This can even affect who stays and who goes during a re-organisation or period of enforced redundancy.

Personal branding may be dismissed as cheesy, cheap or even dishonest. And while most executives recognise its power, some are better at it than others. Certain cultures, particularly those of the English-speaking world, lead the way, sometimes shamelessly. Elsewhere, managers from Asia, Scandinavia and Africa feel uncomfortable putting themselves forward for special attention.

> Personal branding is your reputation and how people perceive you, and what they associate you with.
>
> It conveys an indelible impression that distinguishes you in a unique way. It stems from everything about you, including your appearance, clothing, knowledge, know-how, achievements, reputation and image.

Who you are, what makes you special and making sure others know, affects your chances of success. When Jack Welch, CEO of GE, chose three possible successors in 2000, he told them they had 12 months to show their worth. You can be sure each candidate worked intensely on selling and marketing their personal brand over those next 12 months.

Working on your personal brand can help you understand yourself better. It will also raise your confidence, improve your visibility and even influence your pay. When personal branding works, it leads to more interesting job assignments, and enables people to thrive during tough times.

Three steps to personal branding

Step 1: nail down your brand

Enhancing your personal brand will be a journey, not a destination. It starts with how you see the world and what you want to achieve. The brand you select will be highly personal – there is only one of you. What you regard as your brand must connect to a confident part of your character, the one that builds your personal identity.

The general image of branding is tacky: tawdry TV commercials, excruciating endorsements, and dubious offers. But powerful personal branding relies on authenticity and consistency. Honing your brand demands you are honest about who you are and what you stand for. For instance, if you are funny, outgoing and a free spirit, you will not succeed by presenting yourself as predictable, steady and focused. Likewise, it's no use promoting yourself as wildly innovative or a risk taker when in fact you are deeply analytical, thoughtful and generally cautious.

Attention to your personal brand becomes useful only when you actively communicate it to the right people (see Step 2, page 92). So, who are the right people? Is it just your boss, the entire company or one or two important divisions? Success here stems from focus. For example, to clarify your message can you identify specific people or characteristics of your target audience? Use this tough question that may take some time to answer with confidence:

What makes me different and why should people care?

The answer is not in terms of profession such as 'great accountant', or 'The best CIO you can hire'. Differentiation is what counts. In a world trying to commoditise just about everything, being different matters. It is what makes you unique. You may decide that what makes you special is a combination of talents and experience. When you arrive at a simple message, you have the makings of a strong personal brand.

My unique combination

Think of your education, skills, experience, organisations you have worked in. What have you achieved that is measurable and could be relevant to others, especially employers? Now describe your unique combination in no more than seven short sentences

1 ....

2 ....

3 ....

4 ....

5 ....

6 ....

7 ....

Compare this list with any social media profiles you have posted at networking sites like LinkedIn. Does your online profile fully reflect your unique combination?

If you work in a bank with 8000 employees, you can hardly sum yourself up convincingly as 'the smartest manager in financial services'. But you can find a subtle way to champion a cause or develop a strong area of expertise. It's about getting known for what you do best. Personal branding as a manager requires you to develop new areas of proficiencies that will be prized in the future, such as creativity, coaching, innovation, managing conflict and so on.

Having uncovered what makes you unique, or at least different, the next step is leveraging this. For example, if you are great at metrics, do people know, or are you assuming they know? How could you make sure they do know? This may seem like boasting, or lacking in modesty, but it depends on how you communicate the essence of your brand.

Suppose you are strong on team building. Steering your team may not be enough to also build a personal brand. But people might view you differently if, for example, you initiated a half-day workshop for colleagues on an aspect of team development and shared your experiences. Almost certainly it would tend to raise your profile, at least for a while.

Try writing down and describing your brand. This generally proves stimulating and even revealing. To clarify your brand position might include:

◆ Target market – this might be by niche or by job title

◆ Personal attributes and characteristics that define how I want to be perceived

◆ Specific technical skills I want to highlight for others

◆ A plan to convey to others what makes me different.

Example statements

'I am a dedicated professional who now manages other professionals, able to help owners of small manufacturing businesses develop and execute succession plans that guarantee firm continuity. No other qualified manager with my technical background in the market can combine innovative thinking with resources, contacts and experience like I do.'

'I am a manager who uses the audit process as a stepping-stone to understand and help my tax-exempt clients solve their business issues. My clients think of me as a team player and a "go-to" resource who can find ways to solve their problems.'

'I am a risk specialist with exceptional knowledge in this field and able to deliver insightful and critical advice to clients in urgent need of minimising or eliminating risk to their business. My managers can absolutely rely on me to do more than just lead projects; they know I will constantly look for opportunities to help my team excel.'

As you can see from the above, a brand statement can be either narrow or broad. Your position statement will gradually simplify as you realise the value of your brand. The narrower your market niche the more certain you will become about your target market.

Sample brand statement

John Turner manages a team of psychologists servicing corporate assessment centres. John describes his personal brand like this:

Brand attributes	Analytical thinker, relationship builder, sincere, astute, values driven
Vision	To help talent emerge and for people to fulfil their potential
Purpose	To be proactive in every situation I am involved in, whether business, social, community, and to bring my natural humanity to each project
Values	Integrity, respect, authenticity, fun, relationships, commitment, trust
Powers	Energy, insight, warmth, persistence, confidence, openness
Passions	Family, developing people, friendship and staying in touch, development of sustainable eco systems

Brand ME

Yet another way of clarifying your personal brand is thinking of yourself as a company – Brand Me. In the UK this would be ME plc. Elsewhere it might be ME pte, ME S.A., ME Inc. If you were really a company it would be sensible to clarify:

◆ What are the strengths of ME plc?

◆ Where is ME plc investing in development?

◆ Who are the stakeholders with an interest in the success of ME plc?

◆ What challenges does ME plc currently face?

◆ What plans does ME plc have for the next three years?

◆ In what areas will ME plc be vulnerable?

Now imagine you are journalist from, say, the *Financial Times*, conducting research for a feature on ME plc. Naturally you would ask questions about the nature of this 'company', where it is going and how it is doing. You would probably push to discover uncomfortable facts or problems by asking: Are you investing enough in the development of the company? How is the changing work scene affecting this company? Do stakeholders and other interested parties know enough of the company's achievements? Is there a plan to communicate company successes sufficiently widely? What changes should this company make to ensure it continues to be a success?

Step 2: speak out

The next important step is to promote your brand identity – that is, tell the world, or rather your target audience, you exist and are special. You need to be proactive in conveying this to colleagues, your organisation and the wider world. It means being willing to step into the limelight and demand attention. Your brand will be weak if you are unwilling to make this effort.

the stronger your brand, the less you need to sell yourself

Your personal brand has two dimensions: reputation and reach. You need to be concerned with both. For example, you may have a terrific reputation amongst five people. But what if fifty or five hundred people kept thinking about you?

The stronger your brand, the less you need to sell yourself. Human beings are not products and we cannot always boil them down to a single brand message. As human beings we are far more than that, we are full of nuances. But the nature of brands is to simplify. They rely on a basic meaning, with little room for shades of grey.

Simplification and focus allow you to pursue your personal brand and communicate it consistently to people. This can pay off in various ways, especially in supporting your career prospects. For example, have you ever wondered why some people receive unasked-for lucrative job offers, or are approached by headhunters to consider juicy alternatives? Such people are probably no better qualified or experienced than you. Yet the offers keep coming. These 'lucky' people have managed to nurse their personal brand to the point where they stand out, beyond the day-to-day work they do.

Once you have clarified your brand profile, it is time to use communications tools to reach your audience. Your chosen methods could vary widely and might include speaking engagements, networking, writing articles, volunteering for assignments and so on. You might consider presenting in webinars, contributing thought-leadership pieces to corporate blogs or writing for your firm's e-newsletter.

Social media such as Twitter and Facebook are a mixed blessing for honing a personal brand. Unless you sustain a regular flow of quality communication, it may merely drain your energy and distract you from more useful resources. Professional social media sites, such as LinkedIn, let you promote your profile. Interest groups you join also help you create a visible 'presence'.

Tim Ferriss, a high-profile, US self-branding expert, is enthusiastic about these opportunities: 'Get smart and get real. You, Inc exists whether you want it to or not. Manage your personal brand so you can benefit from the new digital landscape instead of suffering from it.'

Finally, polish your elevator pitch. Imagine entering an empty lift and someone of importance enters. As the doors close on both of you, they ask what you do and who you are. Will your answer be so succinct and clear that when the lift doors re-open 30 seconds later, you leave them with an indelible impression? (See also Chapter 4 Communicate with Impact).

Step 3: evaluate and evolve

You've defined your brand and identified communication tools to reach your target audience. Now, how do you measure your brand's success? One sign, of course, is that you keep getting promoted. Another is attractive offers of employment keep winging your way, or you regularly get invited to speak at conferences.

Use performance evaluations and informal feedback from managers and peers to refine your brand. Find a group of people you trust to give you honest feedback, and use them as your focus group. If you're a consultant, provide your clients with feedback forms after every project. If you run a personal blog or website ask for feedback on it. All strong brands evolve over time and so must yours. To stay relevant means constant refinements and modifying how you communicate the essence of your brand and checking how people perceive it.

A common request made to coaches who provide managers with one-to-one support is: 'How can I raise my profile?' This is an entirely reasonable request, since it may ultimately mean the difference between an unfulfilling job and a rewarding career. Most successful managers constantly re-invent themselves. This can mean seeking new challenges, shifting into more meaningful work or tackling any negative perceptions that could hinder your career progress.

Suppose you have somehow acquired a reputation for being weak with numbers. Protesting you are perfectly at home with metrics and quantification may do little to change this picture. Somehow, you will need to produce creative ways to transform this negative into a positive. For example, you might circulate completion tables, publicise achieved deadlines, or hold celebrations when you or the team hit critical numerical targets. These can all serve to alter your profile, without labelling you as notoriously ambitious.

Do you have enough information about how others see you? Check how the world at large views your brand. If we are mentioned online our brand is already out there, for better or worse. Not being mentioned could imply you are in big trouble. Everyone, from a potential employer to a prospective blind date, can check out your brand online. For example, if you type your first and second name with quotation marks around it into Google, what happens? Out of the first three pages of results showing people with the same name as you, how many entries refer to you? Have fun using the online identify calculator at: **www.onlineidcalculator.com**.

Research commissioned by Microsoft in 2009 found that four out of five US hiring managers and job recruiters reviewed online information about potential job candidates. If someone Googled you, will the information support your brand or undermine it? Researchers also found that most (70 per cent) of US hiring managers rejected candidates based on what they discovered online about that person. These results would almost certainly apply elsewhere.

Many people interpret personal branding as treating themselves like a product. That way lies madness! Personal brands consist of people who are willing to allow their natural talents and strengths to stand out, without manipulation or imitating others. Whether you regard personal branding as cheesy, tiresome or a gross over-simplification of who you are, it is here to stay.

Ways to develop your brand

☐ *Treat the task of continually honing your personal brand as a journey, not a destination – so keep taking actions that ensure it stays fresh and active*

☐ *Use the three step process of 1) Nail down your brand, 2) Speak out and 3) Evaluate and evolve the brand*

☐ *For Step 1 clarify your personal values, purpose and goals – actually write these down, don't just hold them in your head; create a written personal brand-position statement*

☐ *For Step 2 actively promote your personal brand by being willing to step into the limelight and demand attention from the world, using all suitable media to get your message across*

☐ *For Step 3 measure your brand's success – that is, assess how successful you are being at getting your basic message across. If you are unsure what your message is, go back to Step 1!*

☐ *Know the answer to the question: 'What makes you different and why should anyone care?'*

☐ *Focus your energy in promoting your brand – decide what you need to learn, what else do you need to know, how could you learn it and when?*

☐ *To focus your thoughts on your brand, try thinking of yourself as a company – Me plc*

☐ *Conduct a research project on ME plc, or BRAND ME, as a journalist enquiring into this company. Ask penetrating questions about the nature of this 'company' and why it is special and effective*

☐ *As part of Speaking Out, take part in webinars, contribute challenging or thought-leadership pieces to corporate blogs, write for your firm's e-newsletter*

☐ *Decide how you will measure the success of your brand – come up with some metrics or measures that indicate whether your brand is working well enough for you*

☐ *As part of promoting your brand, seek out new challenges, if necessary shift into more meaningful work, tackle any negative perceptions that could hinder your career progression*

☐ *Find a group of people you trust to give you honest feedback, and use them as a focus group to identify how to strengthen your personal brand*

PART 2

Manage others

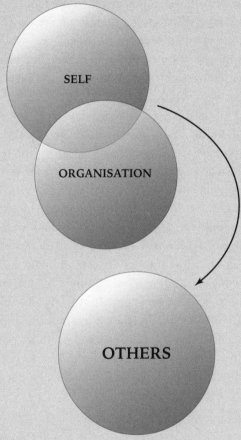

SELF

ORGANISATION

OTHERS

Others

- Show leadership
- Generate team working
- Manage your boss
- Promote engagement
- Coach for results
- Negotiate successfully
- Handle problem people

Managing others requires you to hone your awareness of what they need to be effective, applying your insight to helping them perform at their best, unlocking their potential.

These seven aspects of being a manager focus on key areas where newcomers often struggle to make headway: show leadership; generate team working; manage your boss; promote engagement; coach for results; negotiate successfully; and handle problem people.

You could argue this part encompasses everything management is all about and into which all the rest should fit. Though a legitimate view, if you are starting on the management road the above grouping can prove helpful in nailing down the essentials.

A theme running through this part on managing others is making sure people feel aligned to the corporate strategy and feel fully engaged. The Global Workforce study by Towers Perrin in 2007 brought into sharp focus the extraordinary underused potential of so many people at work. Its survey of 90,000 people across 18 countries found most people at work withhold their full range of abilities. In the UK, for example, a minuscule 14 per cent of employees feel fully engaged with their work and therefore are performing to their maximum. That leaves a huge 86 per cent of people who could perform better. In essence this is what managing others is about.

7

Show leadership

BRIAN PICKED UP THE PHONE to hear his boss asking to see him right away. Slightly anxious about this unexpected summons, he ran down the corridor and was in the other office within half a minute. As usual, his boss had that permanently serious look on his much-lined face.

'Brian, thanks for coming so promptly. Why I called you is quite simple. I want your resignation as a manager.' Brian sat up shocked, and the colour drained from his cheeks. 'What, why? What's gone wrong?'

'Nothing,' replied his manager, obviously relishing the drama, 'I want your resignation as a manager because I need you to start acting as a leader.' The rest of the meeting went by in a blur. But Brian never forgot the day he stopped thinking like a manager and began acting like a leader.

Is there a difference between being a leader and being a manager? The distinction used to be simple to make. Managers implemented and were mainly reactive. They did essential if rather boring things like plan, organise, and make sure the organisation had the right people. In contrast, effective leaders were proactive, anticipated problems, and discovered opportunities. They also did high-level work such as strategic thinking.

You could sum up their job as 'doing what is right, focusing on values, direction and inspiring people'. They were also the ones with charisma.

This neat separation never really made sense. Organisations these days expect their managers also to show leadership; and their leaders to understand and be effective at managing.

The charisma myth

One of the pervasive myths of leadership is the need for a powerful charisma. In fact those running successful, long-lasting organisations differ from the high-profile, larger-than-life personality conventionally associated with top leaders. The most outstanding ones are modest and humble, while also being fearless and determined. That could equally describe many effective managers, who never perhaps consider themselves as leaders in the formal sense.

To show leadership therefore, you do not need to brim with charisma, or cause entire rooms to fall silent when you enter. The three important steps to taking a lead, without actually having a high-level leadership role are:

1 **Position to lead**: create more time for strategy and to obtain information and opinion from beyond the organisation; re-organise the team so you become less central to its everyday tasks.

2 **Share information**: pass on what you learn, especially from customers and other external partners; help reorientate people around goals aligned to your own.

3 **Influence not order:** continue to work *with* colleagues, without lecturing them; view the current situation from their perspective; look for ways to modify and simplify

procedures, rather than replacing them or adding complex new tasks onto them.

Beyond these basics, you also show leadership when you:

◆ select what needs to be done

◆ think about the future and what is right for the organisation

◆ develop action plans

◆ take responsibility for decisions

◆ initiate communication

◆ focus on opportunities rather than problems

◆ run productive meetings

◆ think and say 'we' rather than 'I'

◆ show you care about your people so they develop trust in you.

Running like a thread through all these actions are two strands that allow you to show leadership while still nominally being a manager: you need to be proactive and be authentic. Being proactive means you take initiatives, set examples, volunteer for assignments and make things happen. Each of these can help demonstrate your leadership in highly practical and often visible ways. Being authentic is simply being yourself, doing what you say you will do, and showing integrity.

Select what needs to be done

'I have never encountered an executive who remains effective while tackling more than two tasks at a time,' commented the father of modern management, Peter Drucker, who worked with and advised hundreds of managers over his highly productive life.

To show leadership, amongst other things, is to focus on what matters and set priorities. You will continually face choices involving situations and people demanding your attention. (See also Chapter 3.) Correctly choosing where to put your attention and where to stay focused marks you out as a leader, not just someone who implements what other people ask you to do.

Think about what is right for the organisation

Managers who act like leaders think strategically. They see the bigger picture, which can often be decisive in influencing others. By asking, 'What is right for this organisation?' you show you can reach beyond your immediate area of responsibility and avoid the trap of narrow sectional interests.

thinking strategically is not particularly easy

Thinking strategically is not particularly easy. You probably do not have the full picture and others may even suggest you should not be doing this kind of activity. 'Get back to managing and leave the big issues to us,' is how they might put it, if really pushed. Showing leadership means being willing to step out and being seen to focus on the bigger picture of what is best for the organisation and then acting on it.

Develop action plans

'It's all in my head. I know exactly what should happen and what I want to achieve.' If you are tempted to talk like this, then you risk becoming a prisoner of events. Without a proper action plan in writing, which you can use as a guide and bench mark, you have no real way of knowing which of the events happening around you matter and which do not.

Develop a clear statement of intention, one you are prepared to revise often, talk about constantly and use to make sense of the inevitable and unpredictable opportunities that come your way. The opportunities will doubtless make mincemeat of your intention or, putting it slightly differently, 'To make God laugh talk about your plans.' But creating definite and documented plans in the first place is an important leadership, and certainly management, task.

Take responsibility for decisions

Acting as a leader means holding yourself accountable for essential actions and ones you initiate. Putting it more crudely, you show you are willing to take the blame as well as claiming the credit for success.

Being ready to admit publicly you are wrong, have made the wrong choice, or have made a mistake, can be painful and for some people almost impossible. Yet it is what successful leaders do. They are constantly willing to put themselves on the line, reveal their vulnerability and show they are human and not above messing things up.

Initiate communication

Showing leadership also means you:

◆ make sure action plans are published and fully understood

◆ ask for comments from all colleagues on what needs doing and how

◆ ensure people know what information they need to get the job done

◆ master the information, not letting it master you.

This last requirement is particularly important since the amount of information available is almost infinite. Yet it is seldom more facts that you need: what is vital are knowledge, understanding, interpretation and conclusions.

Focus on opportunities rather than problems

Just about everywhere you look, you will uncover problems. Managers traditionally solve these, spending much of their waking hours coming up with fixes. By contrast, leaders focus more on opportunities and again this can help distinguish you favourably from others around you.

It is not a case of saying, 'Don't bother me with problems, bring me solutions,' which can be an excuse to dump important issues into other people's laps. Instead, you make sure that problems do not overwhelm the opportunities.

Run productive meetings

Every study of what managers actually do confirms that even the newest ones spend more than half their time with other people, that is, in meetings of some kind. Even a conversation with one other person is a meeting.

Effective leaders make their meetings unmissable. They ensure these are work sessions, rather than talking shops or focused exclusively on problems. Show your leadership capability by becoming an expert at running rewarding meetings where people really want to be, rather than merely being required to attend.

Running an effective meeting is not hard, yet it is surprising how many dreadful meetings happen every day in just about every organisation you can find. But it does not have to be like that. (See Chapter 16.)

Think and say 'we' rather than 'I'

You have authority in your organisation because you have gained people's trust. As a leader this means showing clearly that when it comes to your personal needs and opportunities you will put those of the organisation first. This is not at all as easy as it sounds.

It is hard to keep thinking of the organisation rather than your own interests, and many leaders have signally failed to do this. When you say 'we' you show you are putting your ego and your personal desires aside in favour of what is right for your team, your division or the organisation.

Show you care about your people

There are still further practical ways you can demonstrate your leadership, including getting the best from each person, modelling desired behaviour, telling stories, being inspiring and values driven.

Get the best from each person

Be inquisitive about each person who reports to you:

◆ discover what is unique about them

◆ know the individual's strengths

◆ discover the triggers that activate those strengths

◆ identify the individual's learning style.

Great managers who show leadership spend plenty of time away from their desks. They walk around, watch people's reactions to events, listen and take mental notes about what attracts each individual's enthusiasm and what they struggle with.

great managers spend plenty of time away from their desks

How do you discover these sometimes-elusive facts? Mainly by asking! For example, you might identify a person's strengths by asking: 'What was the best day at work you've had in the past three months? What were you doing and why did you enjoy it so much?' A strength is not just something the person is good at. It is also something they find naturally satisfying and they look forward to doing it repeatedly and getting better at it.

Likewise, ask about the worst day the person experienced in recent months. Probe for details about what they were doing and why they disliked it so much.

Despite the importance of self-awareness, showing leadership does not necessarily mean pushing those you manage to be more self-aware, for example by making them aware of their weaknesses. What counts more than self-awareness is their confidence or self-assurance.

Aim to reinforce confidence, to build self-assurance so the person can persist in the face of obstacles, bounce back when reversals occur and eventually achieve the goals they set. Do this by focusing on the person's strengths and praising their successes not in terms of the hard work involved, but in terms of using their strengths. Put more simply, work to create a state of mind filled with optimism so your people can overcome obstacles and achieve results.

Model desired behaviour

Mahatma Gandhi argued, 'You must be the change you wish to see in the world.' As a leader, people look to you to show them the way, to demonstrate by example how they should behave. Modelling desired behaviour is a challenge, yet is one of the most powerful weapons in your management armoury.

By modelling desired behaviour you provide your people with a visible template against which they create their own actions. Using this template, they gain an understanding of how you will judge them. Contrast this with the more common 'don't do as I do, do as I say' approach, which many managers and leaders adopt and then wonder why they have a hard time making things happen.

The more you advance within an organisation the more important modelling desired behaviours becomes, while proving to be more challenging for you personally. Yet it can be one of the most powerful ways in which to exert your leadership.

Tell stories

Strong leaders tend to be great storytellers. They love bringing their messages to life with personal tales, lively examples, and by talking about their experiences or those of others. In other words, they use stories to capture people's attention and then affect their emotions. When a leader tells a good story it can travel at light speed across the organisation, influencing and affecting people at all levels.

a good story can travel at light speed

While it helps to be a natural raconteur, it is more important that you simply develop your natural ability to bring your key messages to life through stories that entertain and grab people's imagination. Show your leadership by actively searching for and sharing relevant stories with people – stories of success, good practice, exemplary behaviour, outstanding performance, someone making a real difference and so on.

Inspire people

The idea that you might need to inspire people may feel daunting and, for most leaders, it can certainly be a challenge. Yet this lies at the heart of getting the best from people, so you may as well start getting to grips with this issue now. It will become increasingly important as your career develops.

Being inspiring is not necessarily about demonstrating a large charisma, though that can sometimes help. It is more concerned with learning to tap into what moves you, then using it to connect with others, affecting them emotionally and in terms of attitude.

Values driven

Successful leaders repeatedly articulate what they regard as really important, such as shareholder value, integrity, respect for the individual, diversity and so on.

When you are values driven people soon understand where you are coming from in your communication and in reaching for goals. While these values may partly be based on ones already identified by the organisation, for instance through its mission statement and other such material, it is also important you know and express your own values, and share these with people.

The important point about values is that they help other people make decisions when you are not there – they set the framework within which actions should take place.

Ways to show leadership

☐ *Select what needs to be done*

☐ *Consider what is right for the organisation*

☐ *Develop action plans*

☐ *Take responsibility for decisions*

☐ *Initiate communication*

☐ *Focus on opportunities rather than problems*

☐ *Run productive meetings*

☐ *Think and say 'we' rather than 'I'*

☐ *Be proactive*

☐ *Discover what is unique about each person, their strengths and how they best learn*

☐ *Reinforce confidence and build self-assurance so people persist in the face of obstacles*

☐ *Show by example what you want people to do*

☐ *Use stories about success, good practice, exemplary behaviour, outstanding performance and so on*

☐ *Learn to tap into what moves you and use this to connect with others*

☐ *Be values driven and talk about what matters most to you*

☐ *Spend plenty of time away from your desk, walking around connecting with people*

8

Generate team working

WHAT DO THESE COMPANIES HAVE IN COMMON: Johnson & Johnson, L'Oréal, Mars Incorporated, Novartis Oncology, Pfizer and Philip Morris USA? According to recent research, they are all firms with great business teams. In these and other successful teams, power no longer stays locked in one place or in one person. Instead, power sharing is what allows the team to meet its current challenges.

Since managing teams is a core management skill, the essential point is that you need to encourage power sharing; for example, allowing leadership to move around and not rest entirely with you.

If you have ever been a member of a poorly managed team you will almost certainly recall it as a miserable and frustrating experience. Like most managers, therefore, you probably wonder how to get the best from your team.

Steps to creating a great team

Effective teams consist of more than the sum of their parts. Strong teams seldom just happen and it is one reason for appointing you as a manager – to build an effective team that produces outstanding performance. The good news is that the team itself will almost certainly want you to succeed.

Step 1 – choosing the team members

Your first step towards establishing a well-run team is choosing who should be in it and who should not. You create a successful team rather than inherit it, and only with the right members can you expect to achieve outstanding performance. Traditionally teams use whoever is available. The best teams, those producing a virtuoso performance, choose members for their skills.

Defining team membership can be messy, as you form and re-form people into different groupings. Finalising membership may be a sensitive political issue and it helps to clarify:

- the core team members – those whose contribution is necessary over an extended period
- the supporting team members – those who help the team do its work effectively without becoming too involved with the work
- the temporary team members – those whose contribution is usually specific and time-bound.

In the short term, you may indeed inherit your team and feel you have limited scope to alter the membership. It is easy to resent this situation, becoming trigger-happy and taking it out on the team itself or on certain individuals. Instead, set out to assess gradually each team member and their performance and, only if necessary, replace them. Make this a last resort, not the first one.

If you have the freedom to pick your entire team, make the most of it and watch for a natural tendency to choose clones of yourself. Clones are people who seem similar to you in background, thinking and even how they talk. Instead, aim for a healthy diversity, in which you obtain the talent you need in whatever form it comes. (See also Chapter 20.)

Step 2 – developing the team

The second step in managing your team well is recognising that it needs to develop. Sharing your power, that is, allowing leadership to move around, will be an important way to encourage the team to move through the essential stages of team development.

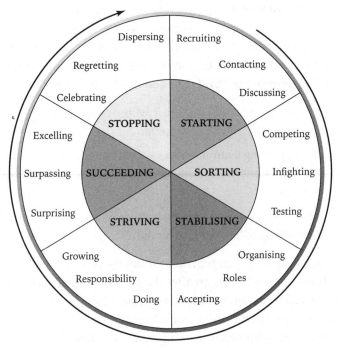

Source: © Maynard Leigh Associates, reproduced with permission.

Some teams complete the stages shown in the diagram above faster than others, especially with skilled help. Consider using an outside team facilitator; one or two days working together can potentially start transforming the group into a more cohesive and effective unit.

Although the stages of starting, sorting, stabilising, striving, succeeding and stopping may blur into one another, at some point every team needs to go through each one. You cannot always expect the team to remain in the succeeding stage since all teams have ups and downs which is why it is so important to keep reviewing how the team views its current performance. Nor can you avoid the stopping stage, since every team has a particular life span and at some point needs to recognise it is time to disband and move on.

Step 3 – coaching and encouraging

The third step towards creating a well-run team consists of clarifying your attitude to the individual members. Do you fully respect them, conveying clearly they are special and worth fighting for? With whom are you most happy to share your power? What would make people feel you should manage them?

Acting as the team coach, rather than trying to be a dominant manager or playing the parental role, is yet another way of sharing power and can prove highly productive. As the team coach, you do less managing, concentrate more on supporting, advising, encouraging and listening. This may mean making time for one-to-ones where you help individual members address how they can be more effective within the team.

acting as the team coach is yet another way of sharing power

Step 4 – becoming a team

The fourth essential step moves your people from being merely a group into becoming a team. Groups tend to be weak in areas in which teams become strong. For example, a powerful team will usually:

◆ accept challenging goals
◆ share values

◆ be interdependent

◆ express feelings

◆ rely on commitment rather than control

◆ demonstrate mutual trust

◆ focus on group processes

◆ regularly work in pairs or small groups.

While some groups may show such behaviour, they seldom do it to the same extent as an effective team.

There are practical actions you can take to encourage these team behaviours:

Encourage acceptance of challenging goals: Successful teams thrive on challenging goals. You can be a stimulus to identifying these, encouraging the team to reach beyond its present achievements. If you simply impose these demanding goals, you risk alienating people. Where possible, make setting team goals a joint exercise in which everyone has their say about what to choose. Chapter 3 deals more fully with setting goals.

Sometimes you may find yourself with a non-negotiable aim, perhaps imposed by those more senior in the organisation. Where possible be frank with the team about these imposed goals, sharing the reasoning behind them. Steer your people towards a creative discussion of *how* to reach these goals.

Describing exactly the way you want the team to achieve the goal risks gaining compliance, rather than a wholehearted genuine commitment to strive for the result. (See also Chapter 3.)

Promote shared values: People who feel strongly about the same things tend to bond together, becoming willing to make allowances for each other. This helps the team become more productive.

Make time during team meetings for development sessions that explore personal values, discovering how these relate to those you want to instil in your team. Again, an outside facilitator may be useful in this area.

Encourage interdependence: In strong teams, members come to rely on each other, knowing they can expect support when facing difficult times or significant challenges. Without interdependence, a group seldom transforms into a team.

Support the growth of interdependence with work assignments and communicate how much you value people working together, rather than always competing with each other. Keep referring to successes as due to team effort, rather than constantly praising individuals for achievements towards which everyone has contributed.

Express feelings: Working in a team means people constantly react with each other with plenty of scope for misunderstandings and communication problems. These start to matter if people cannot share their feelings and express concerns or issues openly.

Perhaps, like many managers, you feel uncomfortable dealing with feelings, including your own. Yet an important sign you are succeeding in managing the team is your ability to handle feelings, particularly strong ones. Some powerful ways to do this are:

- openly acknowledge the existence of feelings

- invite people to talk about them

- during normal meetings make room for feelings to be expressed

- introduce reality checks – do the facts match up with what people are expressing?

Be willing also to show your own feelings. A heartfelt thank you from the boss is worth as much to some employees as a small pay rise. And many people do not feel sufficiently thanked at work, with a significant number saying they never receive thanks.

Push for commitment rather than control: This arises in numerous ways, particularly through a willingness to play together and to spend social time in each other's company. It can also occur through people making that extra effort, or by supporting each other in their work.

One of the best ways to push for commitment is to model it yourself. Demonstrate your willingness to do whatever it takes to get the job done, while working smarter, not harder. So, for example, take the trouble to find resources for a team member, obtain information that people will find useful, and generally do things for the team that show you are making a special effort on their behalf.

You nearly always face a choice between relying on commitment to get things done and exercising managerial control. Strengthen your team by pushing for commitment to achieving results rather than through being in charge. The latter may temporarily make you feel important but long term it can undermine the power of the team to build a culture of success.

encourage the emergence of leaders other than yourself

In winning teams, people thrive on autonomy and challenge, rather than constant direction. It is a difficult balance to strike, but worth pursuing. Encourage the emergence of leaders other than yourself. Strangely, the more you achieve shared leadership the stronger you will become as a manager.

Demonstrate mutual trust: This is slightly different to just showing commitment. Trust emerges from actions that cumulatively suggest reliability or trustworthiness. A well-run team demonstrates this when members know their colleagues will represent them well in meetings, or stand up for them in difficult situations in public.

Demonstrate trust by showing you can let go while others take responsibility and leadership. For example, do you personally need to chair all team meetings or even always be there? How much oversight do you impose on people? Are you willing to let them decide how best to do things while showing your concern is mainly with results?

Focus on group processes: This is the other side of the coin to being strongly concerned with results. You encourage people to give attention to *how* the group functions. So, for example, guide your team to spend time looking at how to improve meetings, ways the group deals with conflict or relates to other teams.

Looking at the team development diagram again – what stage is your team at? What would move it to the next one, until it is really motoring? What processes seem messy or ineffective, such as setting team goals, how people work together on projects or regular reporting?

Create and work in pairs or small groups: Break large challenges into smaller chunks suitable for tackling by two or three team members working together. Encourage this process by suggesting which pairs or members of the team working together might best produce the desired results. The more you become familiar with the team, the more you will be able to encourage the right mix of skills.

Become a great briefer

A Premier League football team meeting only once a year with its coach would not stay on top for long. Likewise, teams in organisations need to meet regularly, and the briefing process helps people work well together. Everyone gets to share what is happening, solve problems, review progress and set new team challenges.

Experienced managers rate team briefings as one of the best ways to communicate with colleagues and hear their views. The team briefing is an information sharing exercise. You disseminate important news, decisions and issues that could affect how the team manages its future.

Briefing well is a managerial skill, since it is easy to turn such sessions into a lecture or leave people feeling shortchanged because there was not enough time to discuss fully the implications. The best briefings are two-way, in which you share information and obtain feedback to help the organisation plan its own long-term future.

Many companies make team briefings part of the culture. They are how the organisation gets things done quickly and are not an optional extra. Companies like Federal Express make such gatherings mandatory and regular. They judge the effectiveness of team managers partly by how good they become at briefing their people.

Briefings need to happen at regular and known intervals, rather than coming unexpectedly only when there is some important announcement. E-mails, video conferences, and webcam conversations can be useful to help with briefing team members but are no substitute for getting the team physically together regularly.

Briefing sessions build your team, strengthen relationships, and promote interdependence and collaborative working. It pays to hone your briefing skills and the best place to start is with careful preparation. When you brief your team, you take centre stage and people want and expect you to shine. Even talented actors need to rehearse their lines, so make time to prepare properly. (See also Chapter 4.)

Review performance

Prime ministers, football managers and even pop groups occasionally need to stand back from the fray and ask the essential question: 'How are we doing?' If you think your team is doing fine, then the team review is like a regular health check. If not, then the team review can be an essential way to start changing the situation for the better.

The longer the team works together the more sensible it becomes to explore the basic issue of 'How are we doing?' Reviews may explore a variety of issues, from 'How do we all feel right now?' to 'What is stopping us hitting our targets?' or from 'How do we generate more business?' to 'How well are our team processes working?' (see box overleaf).

Reviewing performance goes beyond merely checking on progress. It is about actively managing the talent at your disposal. This includes making sure that throughout the team there are high levels of engagement – see Chapter 10: Promote engagement. A useful tool for assessing performance is the team profile. The well-known Belbin system, for example, examines what roles people prefer to play in a team, allowing everyone to explore the implications for team performance.

Regular team reviews

◆ Identify blocks to joint working

◆ Build relationships; resolve interpersonal difficulties

◆ Give the team fresh momentum

◆ Provide new direction

◆ Keep the team fresh

◆ Inspire people

◆ Improve commitment

◆ Help understand what is happening

◆ Revive a thirst for growth and change

◆ Refocus attention on the big picture

A different approach builds a picture of actual team performance by combining team members' perceptions of how well
the group is doing. To describe a successful team, for example,
the Maynard Leigh Associates ACE Team Profile relies on 10
essential team processes. Many large organisations use this for
obtaining a frank assessment of the team's performance. Each
team member fills in an online questionnaire and the combined
entries create a visual profile of the team's current performance.

The team profile and separate ones for each team member
highlight where the team is strong and where it may need to
concentrate development effort. Encouraging the team to
engage in this kind of reflection can help establish you as a
thoughtful and challenging team leader. For more about the
ACE Team profile, see **www.maynardleigh.co.uk/our-services/
on-line-services/**.

The ACE team profile

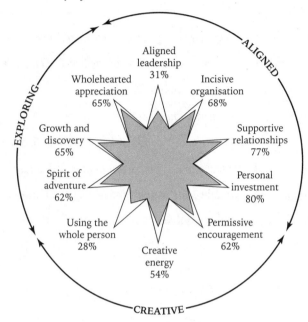

Source: © Maynard Leigh Associates, reproduced with permission.

Ways to manage your team

☐ *Check you have the right people in the team*

☐ *Make replacing a team member your last resort, not the first one*

☐ *Help teams to actively go through the six stages of team development*

☐ *See yourself as the team coach, rather than a dominant manager*

☐ *Help the team to choose challenging goals*

☐ *During team meetings make time to explore personal values*

☐ *If necessary, use outside facilitators to promote team growth and change*

☐ *Arrange work assignments to generate interdependence*

☐ *To promote team openness, be willing to show your own feelings*

☐ *Allow leadership to move around the team*

☐ *Find ways to demonstrate that you trust the team*

☐ *Encourage attention and discussion on how the group functions*

☐ *Divide work so a few team members can jointly work on an issue*

☐ *Become skilled at delivering regular, interesting team briefings*

☐ *Review team progress regularly*

9
Manage your boss

DURING 2008, UK MEMBERS OF PARLIAMENT lambasted BAA's chief executive Colin Mathews over the Terminal 5 fiasco at Heathrow. He publicly admitted he was 'not aware' of problems in the run up to the launch of the multi-billion-pound facility. Shortly afterwards, the airport's managing director who reported to Mathews resigned, following a downgrading in a management reshuffle. The manager paid the price, not only for the debacle, but also for not keeping his boss fully informed.

Four critical mistakes new or inexperienced managers make in boss management are:

1 Being excessively compliant – 'I just need to do what the boss wants'.

2 Demonising – 'I don't trust her/him'.

3 Being target obsessed – 'I'm bound to succeed if I consistently hit my targets'.

4 Being relationship blind – 'All that matters is getting the job done'.

These are negative behaviours. Equally there are some positive behaviours that will help you manage upwards. These include: manage expectations, under-promise and over-deliver, anticipate, and invest in the relationship.

Manage expectations

Passively assuming you know instinctively what the boss wants could create problems. Explore actively the other person's expectations, if necessary asking them to spell out clearly what they want.

Some superiors can convey their expectations simply, others cannot. If necessary, seek a meeting where you jointly examine the whole issue of expectations. You may have to lead the way with direct questions such as:

◆ 'What results are you expecting from me this next quarter?'

◆ 'What would make you feel I was being really effective in this job?'

◆ 'What kind of problems do you want to be informed about and when?'

◆ 'What information do you need before the project is completed?'

Getting a person who tends to be vague to express their expectations can be hard work. Try drafting a detailed note covering the key aspects and send it for their approval. Follow this up with a request for a face-to-face discussion in which you go over each item. This kind of discussion will often bring to the surface expectations, such as:

◆ 'I want you to deliver agreed results on time and show a degree of leadership while doing so.'

◆ 'I need to be kept fully informed about what you are doing.'

◆ 'I expect to be told of any new issues or situations you encounter that might affect my own role or effectiveness.'

◆ 'I rely on you to be my ears and eyes across the division.'

◆ 'You're great at dealing with people, I depend on you to give me early warning if someone or the team feels unhappy about the way things are going.'

Whatever the expectations, it is your job to unravel them, becoming as clear as you can about them. For example, you may need to become assertive and challenge the boss about the urgency of a request with, 'Let me show you my current to-do list so we can agree what to remove from it to allow me to deliver on this timescale.'

Just as the boss will have expectations, you will have some of your own and what you want from the relationship. For example, you may consider it essential to have a regular weekly or monthly meeting to review progress and share useful information. Or you may need extra support when trying to deliver a particularly difficult result. Share these expectations. Do not assume the other person somehow already knows them.

Under-promise and over-deliver

While getting the job done may not be the sole concern of your boss (see above), it will still play a vital part in how well you work together. Make it a personal rule to under-promise and over-deliver.

The results you commit to delivering will normally stem from one or more discussions. Occasionally, though, you may find yourself facing a non-negotiable goal, chosen and imposed by someone else. Externally set *you may find yourself facing a non-negotiable goal* goals, such as sales targets, can be uncomfortable, even oppressive. But, unless you are willing to resign, somehow you will probably end up attempting to reach them.

What counts is making a genuine attempt to succeed, going that extra mile, doing everything possible to deliver – and being seen to do that.

Anticipate

Successful managers thrive by being ahead of the game, anticipating demands and guessing correctly what their bosses want next from them. You do not need to be a mind reader to do this.

- ◆ Become familiar with how the other person thinks and behaves.
- ◆ Stay alert to what is happening around you.
- ◆ Discover issues and problems your boss is currently experiencing.
- ◆ Keep the boss informed.

Look for evidence of what the boss seems most concerned about and then seek opportunities to discuss this. For example, if you realise your boss is anxious about some issue, what contribution could you make to help reduce this concern? Simply being a good listener may be all that you need do in some cases. If you realise that before attending a regular senior meeting your boss tends to fuss excessively, demanding lots of information, you could enquire well in advance whether there is anything you can do to help.

Finally, keep the boss fully informed and avoid surprises.

Invest in the relationship

Otherwise talented managers sometimes ignore the crucial importance of nurturing the boss–subordinate relationship. This is a more subtle game than it might appear. For example, it includes helping to make your boss look good. And in a matrix organisation it could mean finding ways to make your boss's bosses look good. For this you may have to do some market research. For example, you are probably only a LinkedIn connection or a blog comment away from insights into both your boss and their boss. Think of your boss as a brand. How would you sell this to others?

Making your boss look good may simply involve doing things to help this person sparkle. For instance, if you discover the boss's boss likes humour injected into presentations, then you could prepare a project review for your own boss that includes the odd cartoon. Or, if you come across some favourable comments about the boss's boss in an article or a tweet, you could pass this on to your boss, suggesting they bring it to their boss's attention.

Creating a compatible relationship with your boss means clarifying each other's strengths and making up for each other's weaknesses. If you know your boss is weak on follow-through, offer to do this yourself, or provide regular monitoring reports. Discovering what pressures your boss currently faces is not being nosy. It shows you want to be supportive and to help in times of adversity.

If you have been used to having a good, understanding boss, it can be a shock to encounter one who is not. However, this may not just be due to a clash of personalities. The cause may result from different work styles. For instance, you may need to adjust your approach if the other person prefers to receive written reports, rather than talk with you about an issue. Equally, if your boss is a listener, it may be best to deliver a verbal briefing, backed up by a brief written report, e-mail or memo. Unrealistic expectations can undermine the relationship, which is why it is worth spending time getting clear on what each of you expects from the other.

The organisation has a big stake in your boss succeeding, so going over their head must be a last resort. If this seems the only route forward, make sure you pick an issue of real significance to the organisation and not just to get your way, or to win points. (See also below.)

Take the initiative

From your boss's perspective, knowing you do not always wait passively to receive orders can be reassuring. It builds trust and mutual reliance. If you feel you need permission before you can do anything out of the ordinary, it suggests the relationship needs some serious attention.

If something goes wrong, offer your own solutions first – do not wait to be found out. Admittedly, this carries risks as some bosses hate hearing bad news and only want to know when things are going well. This merely means you need to find ingenious ways to get the information across in an acceptable form.

There is a considerable difference, though, between taking the initiative and becoming a loose cannon where your actions are unpredictable and cause unnecessary problems. When using your initiative take time to inform the boss about your actions, inviting comments or discussion about your intentions.

Few things are more disabling for a boss than having a subordinate who is undependable, whose work cannot be trusted. When you take the initiative, it needs to be within the context of delivering the agreed goals, rather than going off on some new direction of your own choosing.

Dealing with an out-of-control boss

Almost everyone has times when the boss seems to have gone crazy. Usually it is a one-off or temporary situation, due to office politics or a personal crisis. But sometimes the resulting behaviour may threaten your team, department or even the company. So what do you do when the boss becomes a problem person?

The reason for being out of control hardly matters. In this uncomfortable situation, the most sensible goal is damage limitation, with clients, employees, suppliers and others. Most of all you want to ensure your work and results continue.

You are almost certainly not alone in seeing the issue. Others also experiencing the problem boss could be subordinates, peers or those higher up the line. Action you can take includes the following.

Prioritise and get on with the work

Do not get distracted with all the ramifications of this problem person. Instead, focus on rallying your team, keeping the boss informed about work problems. Meanwhile take cautious soundings to check whether key influencers like HR people and other functional heads are aware of what is going on.

Raise the issue intelligently

When the boss is reasonable and functioning normally, it is easy to put forward your position and raise problems. It takes courage to do this when the boss has become a problem person and off balance. Colleagues and team members could see doing nothing as weakness.

Control the grapevine

Until the boss recovers, leaves or otherwise changes for the better, remain supportive. Do not give others details, they will know soon enough about the problems. Much the same goes for suppliers and customers: be circumspect about what you say and how you say it.

Know your limit

A problem boss can make life hell and you need to set a deadline on how long you will continue working with this person.

a problem boss can make life hell

Weak managers let this issue drift and consequently may end up suffering for months, even years. What matters is being proactive, which might include organising a move to a boss elsewhere in the same organisation, joining a project team where your boss has less direct power over you or even making plans to leave.

Sit it out

You may decide that because your boss will soon leave or retire, the best strategy is to sit it out and wait. Depending on the timescale, this will be viable only if it does not adversely affect how peers and senior colleagues will judge you.

Initiate contact further up the line

Like resignation, this is almost certainly a last resort strategy and high risk. Do it only when everything else has failed. Top management has a substantial stake in your boss so consider extremely carefully the political ramifications of bypassing your immediate manager.

If you decide to go up the line, present your case in terms of impact on the bottom line; stick to the facts and make no sweeping accusations; do not ask that 'something be done'. (See also Chapter 13.)

Ways to manage your boss

- ☐ *Discover how your boss sees their current goals and pressures*
- ☐ *Make sure you know the person's strengths and weaknesses*
- ☐ *Develop actively and maintain the relationship*
- ☐ *Clarify mutual expectations*
- ☐ *Keep your boss informed*
- ☐ *Avoid seeking help with trivial issues, use your boss's time sparingly*
- ☐ *Become a coach to your manager*
- ☐ *Value your boss's political capital and use it sparingly*
- ☐ *Under-promise and over-deliver*
- ☐ *If you cannot meet a deadline say so sooner rather than later*
- ☐ *Even if you can do your boss's job, do not go around boasting about it*
- ☐ *Respond to questions and treat them with respect*
- ☐ *Do not broadcast your boss's failings*
- ☐ *Defuse criticism or personal attacks with your sense of humour*
- ☐ *Offer solutions not problems*
- ☐ *Show you're a chooser rather than a blamer*
- ☐ *Offer ways to get the best out of yourself; don't have it dragged out of you*
- ☐ *Recognise the relationship reflects mutual dependency and honesty*

10

Promote engagement

YOUR BOSS ENTERS WEARING one of those 'I've got news for you' smiles. Something tricky is coming down and it may not all be good news. She has a stark message. 'We need an increase in profits, greater productivity, and to reduce staff turn-over. Let me have your thoughts by the end of the week please.'

Now it is your turn. A few days later, with a hint of a smile you plonk on her desk a report in a huge bound folder. 'Here's my report. Let me know what you think.' As she opens the first page, you enjoy seeing her eyes widen. Printed on the first page are three large words, all remaining pages are blank. The three words read: 'Increase levels of engagement.'

There is now compelling, worldwide evidence that engagement affects individual and company performance. Almost everywhere and regardless of cultures or country, an essential management skill is grasping the basics of engagement and how to make it happen.

Once, being a manager meant you were a motivator, it was something you did to people just to get them to perform. On that score scientists have long ago clarified some of the essentials. Yet, the lessons have not been widely applied. As Daniel Pink, author of *Drive*, which unravels the whole world of motivation, argues, '... most businesses haven't caught up with the new understanding of what motivates us'. Too many organisations, he suggests, still operate from old-fashioned, unexamined assumptions about human potential and individual performance. What goes on is based more on folklore than on science.

The folklore is that carrots and sticks – money and other external rewards – bring about high levels of performance. The overwhelming evidence from research refutes this. Money, for example, in an increasing number of jobs is not highly motivating, regardless of the myths of bankers' bonuses and so on.

Carrots and sticks, however, seem to work for purely routine work. But there is a steadily decreasing amount of this to manage. Instead, intrinsic motivation – the rewards that come from within – will be far more effective for a growing proportion of the work you manage. Routine work can be outsourced or automated. In contrast, non-routine work demanding thought, imagination, empathy and a creative response will almost certainly become the main focus of your management time.

Essentials of engagement

Organisations, therefore, expect more from their managers than just the raw application of carrot and stick type behaviour. To get to grips with the implications, here are three essentials:

1 Assume people come to work to succeed, not to screw up

2 See your job as a talent manager – uncovering and mobilising talent

3 Ensure each person you manage is fully engaged and inspired.

Assuming people come to work to succeed and not fail affects how you respond to setbacks. These include troublesome behaviour, missed goals and other disappointments about performance. Rather than focusing on the problems, concentrate on causes and how to alter the outcome next time.

by seeing yourself as a talent manager you start to acquire an agenda for action based upon exploiting people's ability to make a difference

By seeing yourself as a talent manager you start to acquire an agenda for action based upon exploiting people's ability to make a difference. Because organisations are increasingly complex, their long-term success depends on encouraging individuals to produce ideas, creative solutions and offer alternative ways of thinking and being. So important is this requirement becoming that many have established the role of talent manager, dedicated to ensuring the organisation keeps focused on unlocking people's potential. Amongst the implications are more attention on succession planning, personal development plans, new ways of recruiting and hiring, and on helping people manage their careers.

What is engagement?

It's when employees feel a close connection with and a commitment to the company's success. It happens when they try to perform at their best and are willing to go the extra mile, beyond basic job requirements. Engaged employees stay for what they can give, the disengaged stay for what they can get.

Engaging facts

◆ Raising engagement by 10 per cent generates an extra £1500 profit per employee annually.

◆ Disengagement cost the UK economy up to £65bn in 2008.

◆ UK companies with worse than average employee engagement suffer 62 per cent more accidents, 230 per cent more employee sick days and 50 per cent more inventory shrinkage.

◆ Managers at companies in the UK with average engagement or worse, spend more than 200 per cent more time dealing with discipline and re-recruitment.

◆ Firms with high engagement levels had total shareholder return that was 19 per cent higher than average in 2009. Low engagement ones had total shareholder return 44 per cent below average.

◆ Engagement surveys without visible follow-up may actually decrease engagement levels.

Sources include: UK Institute of Employment studies; Gallup; Engaging for Success, government report; Global Engagement Report, Blessing White, 2011.

Promoting engagement

To promote engagement amongst your team or those you manage, people need VIDI – to feel valued, involved, developed and inspired:

Source: *Talent Engagement: How to Unlock People's Potential*, Maynard Leigh Associates, 2010, reproduced with permission.

Valued

As we have already noted, this is not all about money. All the available evidence suggests money is not the most important way in which we feel valued at work. For example, few people leave for another job solely because of a salary increase. Therefore, make it your business to learn what is important in the lives of your direct reports, in teams you manage, and for others such as colleagues and peers.

Of the many ways you can contribute to your people feeling valued at work, three of the most important are: respect their individuality; build relationships; and ensure fairness, which includes pay and appreciation.

Involved

Our need for connection and sense of belonging drives us to form relationships of all types, both at work and in our private lives. But we also need to feel that our individuality makes an impact. Engagement often stems from being actively involved in what's going on. How you communicate (see Chapter 4) plays a critical role in whether those on the receiving end feel involved. For example, according to Towers Perrin, only 31 per cent of employees feel that their senior managers communicate openly and honestly.

Three areas that contribute to your people feeling involved at work are: how you promote communications; producing an impact in which you build connections and partnership; and turning work into play.

Developed

As children we cannot help but develop. Why should this stop when we reach adulthood? Growing and developing is a natural human drive. So, when a manager focuses on someone's development it is a powerful way of engaging them. Yet, only about one in three employees get to discuss their training and development needs with their managers. Feedback on performance is equally rare according to Kingston University. (See below – performance management.) Each person in your team needs a proper development plan that they themselves have helped to create. Make a commitment also to provide time to coach them, so they can reach for a new level of performance.

Three areas that contribute to your people feeling developed at work are: focusing on unlocking potential; conducting regular reviews; and providing opportunities for people to experiment and take responsibility.

Inspired

This is perhaps the most challenging aspect of managing engagement. What will it take to get people excited and tap into their natural enthusiasm? How can you best encourage their imagination about ways to improve performance? You cannot inspire others without first being inspired yourself. To connect with your own sources of inspiration, start making a list of all the things that uplift or excite you: people, poems, songs, art, landscapes, events, films, stories, achievements, books.

Be willing to share these sources with colleagues. Talk with passion or vigour about what you feel matters at work. Being a successful manager is not best done by becoming emotionless, or super-objective, immersed in logic and metrics. Sharing what matters to you is a sign of strength, not an indication of weakness. Three ways you can contribute to people feeling inspired at work are: when you act as someone of substance – for example, by promoting integrity, values and the importance of passion; when you encourage the use of imagination; and when you check that work has meaning for people.

Two aspects of generating engagement that deserve special attention are: promoting autonomy; and conducting regular reviews of people's performance.

Autonomy

If there is a clear trend in the area of motivation and engagement, it is towards self-direction. The old idea that people need a prod if they are to perform adequately has diminishing relevance. Practical experience shows it is far more effective to rely on people's natural curiosity and wish to direct their own destiny.

For some management experts, like Daniel Pink and Garel Hamel (see introduction to the first edition), even the word 'management' itself is now obsolete. It should be consigned to the linguistic scrap heap. Instead we need a fundamental shift towards self-direction – that is, what people do, when they do it, how they do it and with whom they do it.

one of the main causes of stress at work is when people feel they have little control over their work or what is happening to them

One of the main causes of stress at work is when people feel they have little control over their work or what is happening to them. Even in areas of high poverty people seek out some sense of autonomy. Meanwhile, a wealth of research confirms that people working in self-organised teams generally perform better and are more satisfied than those who have been forced together managerially.

In summary, autonomy is an essential component of a high level of engagement.

Peformance management

In many workplaces the answer to the perennial engagement question 'how am I doing?' seems to be 'we would rather not tell you!' Too many managers resist conducting performance reviews. Such resistance is not entirely irrational since, in their older form, appraisals are notorious for being a punitive, top-down control device with a long history of failure.

Also behind the resistance to appraisals lies a fear that direct reports will react to even the mildest comment with stone-walling, anger, or tears. Subordinates too worry they will hear only criticism. The result? Everyone keeps quiet, saying as little as possible. The formal annual review therefore has few friends. Critics label it 'one of the seven deadly sins of management' and one even calls it 'a modern-day bloodletting'.

For example, prior to a cultural overhaul at the retailer John Lewis, managers there were overprotective and tolerant of poor performance. In the words of one senior executive: 'It was neither kind nor honest, since it was not giving employees the chance to improve their performance and pay, or generate the careers they wanted.' Reviews, though, are an essential part of producing high levels of engagement and there are some basic ways to ensure that your reviews succeed (see box below).

---

10 ways to make your performance management succeed

◆ Focus on a holistic approach in which engagement is the main objective, not analysing past behaviour.

◆ Regular: reviews should be frequent.

◆ Purpose: establish a clear purpose, i.e. a continuous process of performance improvement.

◆ Prepare: invest in getting ready for each encounter.

◆ Goal setting: encourage people to set their own goals.

◆ Forward looking: focus on the future not the past.

◆ Frankness: be honest and straightforward in giving feedback.

◆ Two-way: be willing to learn how you're doing in managing.

◆ Make it real: make the process evidence based.

◆ Make it logical: give the process a clear structure.

◆ Use self-assessment: trust people to share their view of their performance.

The shift from appraisal to performance management is not merely a change in terminology. It alters your role from what sociologists would term 'critical parent', to a more adult one in which you talent manage. With performance management you focus on continuous performance improvement, not past failures. When you manage performance, the specific results you want include: improved role clarity; linking personal and organisational objectives; setting performance-linked rewards; and in some cases removing poor performers. With such wide-ranging aims, expecting to concentrate this in one or two (usually stressful) appraisals is almost bound to fail.

To avoid your performance management events being a turgid exercise in box ticking or form filling, you will need to embrace the value of performance management. This is more holistic: a total approach to engaging people. It may mean reviewing, for example, the extent to which a person fully sub-scribes to current corporate values and demonstrates this by their actions. It could also mean returning to basics in which the encounters reflect good communication and good one-to-one conversations.

Some of the essentials of effective performance manage-ment are now well established and include encounters that are: simple; regular; purposeful; well prepared; strategic; based on goals; frank; two-way; grounded in reality; logical; and promote self-assessment.

Simple

Studies show that both managers and employees are often confused about too many aims and elements of the perform-ance management procedure. Keep your encounters simple and easy to understand as to their purpose.

Regular

A single annual appraisal makes little sense. If this is how your organisation operates, underpin it with your own, more frequent sessions to review performance and give feedback on 'how you are doing.' Once performance management becomes the norm, not the exception, it can evolve into a mutually satisfying and creative experience. During it you regularly explore how best to help someone excel, to unlock their potential. Focus on specifics, like what support they need to develop, and also cover broad issues such as where the person is heading in their career.

Purposeful

The notorious annual appraisal will usually cover not just past performance, but future expectations and issues of remuneration. No wonder people hate them!

Purpose of Performance Review Systems
Perceived importance vs actual experience

Sample: 926 private and public sector managers

Source: *Performance Review: Balancing Objectives and Content.* M. Strebler, D. Robinson, S. Bevan (2003) Institute of Employment Studies.

Get clear on the purpose of the meeting and explain it fully to the other person. The more explicit the aim, the greater the chance the performance management session will be productive. Encourage questions about it, rather than suggesting you are merely following a set of standard rules.

Well prepared

It is hardly surprising that traditional appraisals have a terrible reputation, since those on the receiving end often face ill-prepared and anxious managers going through the motions. Faced with the prospect of an ordinary appraisal many people say they would rather visit the dentist or fill in a tax return.

> *faced with the prospect of an ordinary appraisal many people say they would rather visit the dentist or fill in a tax return*

Performance management works best if you take the process seriously and prepare well for the event. This means spending time gathering facts and anticipating the sorts of questions each person might want to ask you.

Consider how you can make the performance management event into a powerful and useful conversation. This means being ready to offer direction, rather than pass judgement; to recognise and reward, rather than criticise or punish. Good preparation will steer you towards uncovering employee concerns rather than telling them your concerns. You will find this approach better than ticking boxes or scoring the person on some dubious rating system. In this way you become a leader, facilitator, negotiator, counsellor and even researcher.

Strategic

One thread that should run through each performance management encounter is checking that individual objectives continue to support the organisation's strategy, its mission and values. In essence you ask: 'Is this person supporting our culture and our core aims?' The clear link to organisational purpose is critical to making performance management effective.

Based on goals

You will achieve a higher level of engagement from your people by allowing them control over their goals – see also above on Autonomy. While it may be tempting to hand out goals and deadlines, instead encourage them to select their own. Generally, the evidence suggests they will be far tougher on themselves than you will be! (See also Chapter 3: Deliver under pressure.)

By focusing on goals, you make your performance management encounter forward-looking, rather than trying to unravel past performance. Certainly, share any problems of performance so far, but concentrate on the future by focusing on *aspirations*. Start with the individual's own and how they see themselves developing. Relate these to what the organisation wants to achieve.

Frank

Most of us would rather avoid telling someone they have performed badly. This reluctance explains why people so often view appraisals with contempt. According to research by YouGov, on behalf of Investors in People in the UK, nearly half think their bosses evade home truths when conducting an annual assessment. Almost one in four say the process is unfair.

Your performance review meetings must therefore strike a balance between some attention to the past and how the person performed, and looking forward to future performance. Rely on openness and frankness to win people's interest in their review.

Two-way

The ideal performance management that fully engages people will be a genuinely two-way experience, a year-round dialogue between you and the employee. This requirement puts more demands on you than simply telling someone how they have been doing. It means inviting feedback about your own effectiveness as a talent manager. In effect you ask: 'how am I doing at getting the best from you?' By making the review experience a two-way event, you gain invaluable information about how you can be more effective as a manager and leader. For example, you may fondly believe you are accessible and easy to reach. With a genuine two-way exchange you may discover people find you less available than you think. Or you may believe you give clear instructions for work tasks, only to learn in the exchange that you could be much clearer.

As part of encouraging a two-way conversation, give the other person a chance to prepare for the encounter. Explain in advance that when you meet you want to hear from them where they find you strong or weak in helping them perform their job well. This moves the review away from blaming company problems on individuals, to focusing on the quality of the management they receive. Also, if you only deal with the individual's issues without the wider company context, you may simply damage morale.

Grounded in reality

performance management works best when based on evidence

Performance management works best when based on evidence. Vague assertions such as 'you could try harder', or 'you have the wrong attitude' will undermine the review and build resistance to hearing more positive feedback. Without evidence that people can understand, you risk accusations of bias, of being uninformed about the person's actual performance, or of relying on hearsay.

Be active in seeking out these solid facts. Dig out examples from peer assessments, discussions with colleagues, rating scales, testing competencies and comparing individual results against agreed goals. People relish concrete examples of good or bad behaviour, attitudes or choices.

Logical

Well-run reviews usually adopt a definite structure. In this way both parties know the territory you will be covering and a typical structure might be:

◆ Introduction – *'How we are going to go about this together?'*

◆ Discuss performance strength – *'Where have you done really well?'*

◆ Review areas for personal development – *'Which areas of performance are to improve or develop?'*

◆ Identify new goals or modify existing ones.

◆ Create specific plans – *'What action to set in motion and by when?'*

◆ Summarise – *'The key points we have discussed and agreed.'*

What matters is creating a logical progression, moving from one issue to the next in a planned way. Such an approach gives reassurance that you will not skate over or miss out anything important. Start the whole process with a written agenda, and to complete it allow at least 60–90 minutes. Follow up with a written report detailing the decisions. Give the other person an opportunity to comment on it.

Encourage self-assessment

Self-assessment is a powerful way to engage people and encourage shared responsibility for performance management. However, this can be challenging, particularly if the person has never previously received useful feedback. First, invite them to consider the elements of their job they feel to be the most important. Secondly, invite them to seek feedback from colleagues, subordinates, and customers. For example, can they recall both negative and positive examples of how people reacted to them in recent meetings, or whether people seem pleased to interact with them, either one-to-one or in groups?

A self-generated review helps the person internalise the results: that is, they begin making use of the information about their performance. Because some people may be shy or reluctant to speak about strengths and overplay their weaknesses, encourage a balanced discussion about strengths and re-frame weaknesses in a positive way: *'It's true you say little in meetings, but you always seem to give everyone your full attention.'*

Use active listening (see Chapter 2) to detect repeated statements or key words that might reveal an important issue and confirm you have correctly understood, or seen its importance. Summarise key points and ask if you have understood the issues.

Finally, compare the person's own perception of their performance with your own view of it. This is when you offer your balanced picture of their strengths and developmental needs.

Ways to promote engagement

☐ *Act as a talent manager to unlock people's potential to excel*

☐ *Encourage engagement so that people feel valued, involved, developed and inspired*

☐ *Discover people who are important in the lives of your direct reports*

☐ *Each person in your team needs a proper development plan they helped to create*

☐ *Find time to coach people to reach new performance levels*

☐ *To inspire others, first become inspired yourself*

☐ *Show people how they are doing in their work, answering the question 'how am I doing?'*

☐ *Use the 10 simple principles of successful performance management reviews*

- *Review performance regularly and frequently*

- *Establish a clear purpose for the review*

- *Prepare well for each session*

- *Encourage people to set their own performance goals*

- *Make the conversation forward, not backward looking*

- *Adopt a frank approach*

- *Two-way*

- *Make it real*

- *Make it logical*

- *Use self-assessment*

11

Coach for results

THE JOKES JUST KEEP COMING. Everyone in your team laughs, but in a rather strained way since the humour usually comes at someone's expense. You could tell the team comedian to stop it, hoping a gentle slap-on-the-wrist will work. But what if the jokes continue? The joker in your team would be a prime candidate for one-to-one coaching, helping them to use their abundant humour more appropriately. As a way of improving people's performance, coaching is now widely accepted as a core skill for virtually all managers.

coaching is now widely accepted as a core skill

You may need to coach at any time, offering coaching to virtually anyone who values your support, including your boss. It also differs in important ways from everyday management. While managers provide direction and make the best use of resources, as a coach you focus on showing people how they can do it themselves. It is the equivalent of teaching someone to fish, rather than merely handing over dead fish.

The best management coaches focus on achieving specific results usually based around improving work performance. Coaching involves a less hierarchical relationship than the managerial one, and it's less directive. It is more like a carefully arranged conversation, based on mutual respect with a shared wish to grow and develop. The quality of the conversation determines whether you make any difference to the person's actual behaviour.

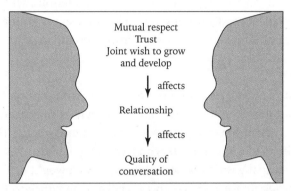

Source: *Be a High Performance Coach: A Solutions Guide.* © Maynard Leigh Associates, 2005, reproduced with permission.

Unlike managing change in the broader organisational sense (see Chapter 14), the power of coaching lies in helping to change an individual's behaviour to improve their effectiveness. Quite simply, when you coach well you help people understand how to succeed.

The mentor versus coach relationship is shown in the table below.

Mentor	Coach
Ongoing and long-term	Short-term focus
Recipient describes need	Coach may suggest needs
Teacher	Trainer
Not directly accountable	Directly accountable if a line manager
Works on personal and professional issues	Concentrates on job-related issues

I don't want to coach!

While every manager needs to learn to coach for results, not everyone takes to the idea of coaching. Many find it time-consuming and regard the process as mysterious, with uncertain outcomes. Reluctance to coach often stems from a fear of being candid, and inadequate personal boundaries.

Candour

To be a good coach you need to be frank with the other person about their performance. Candour, though, can generate emotion, which for some managers feels intensely scary. The best antidote to this fear starts with respecting the other person. Do they actually want you to be candid? When would be the most appropriate time to give them feedback on which to base the coaching conversation? In what form would they find factual feedback most useful – for example, as questions, as straight information, as stories?

Personal boundaries

Fear of overstepping personal boundaries also explains resistance to being a coach. For example, it may feel like assuming too much responsibility for someone's performance. 'I'm a manager, not a therapist' is how some people justify avoiding the coaching role. Yet good coaching is about discovery, not therapy. It uses many of the skills of basic management, including emotional intelligence (EI), listening, questioning, persuasion, goal setting and managing meetings.

As a coach, by focusing on results you strengthen the boundaries around the conversation held with the other person. You do not try to change their personality, only how they go about producing results at work.

Outside help

You could consider outsourcing the job to a specialist. But not being able to coach for results may eventually damage your career. As you progress, you will be increasingly working with people who you cannot command what to do. To obtain the best from them will mean adopting a coaching style. (See also Chapter 13.)

The five stages

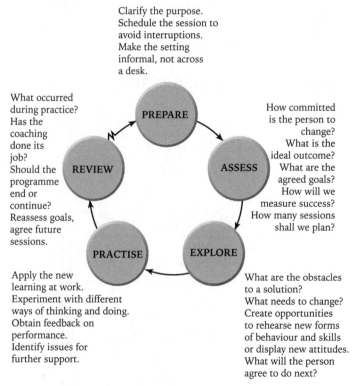

Clarify the purpose.
Schedule the session to
avoid interruptions.
Make the setting
informal, not across
a desk.

PREPARE

How committed
is the person to
change?
What is the
ideal outcome?
What are the
agreed goals?
How will we
measure success?
How many sessions
shall we plan?

ASSESS

What occurred
during practice?
Has the
coaching
done its
job?
Should the
programme
end or
continue?
Reassess goals,
agree future
sessions.

REVIEW

PRACTISE

Apply the new
learning at work.
Experiment with different
ways of thinking and doing.
Obtain feedback on
performance.
Identify issues for
further support.

EXPLORE

What are the obstacles
to a solution?
What needs to change?
Create opportunities
to rehearse new forms
of behaviour and skills
or display new attitudes.
What will the person
agree to do next?

Source: *Be a High Performance Coach: A Solutions Guide.* © Maynard Leigh Associates, 2005, reproduced with permission.

You may find it useful to attend a development workshop. This will allow you to practise coaching safely and discover its power. Think of it as a five-stage process: prepare, assess, explore, practise and review.

These various stages need not be complicated or lengthy. But they can make the coaching process more systematic, predictable and for the person on the receiving end more reassuring. The five-stage process is particularly useful when you conduct formal coaching activity, perhaps over several months.

It is worth explaining to the other person the various stages of how coaching works. This allows them to adjust their expectations, giving them confidence in you – you know the journey on which you are taking them.

Action-focused coaching (AFC)

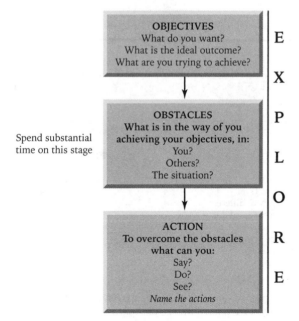

Source: *Be a High Performance Coach: A Solutions Guide.* © Maynard Leigh Associates, 2005, reproduced with permission.

A short, informal, coaching session may not need the full five-stage approach: for instance, when you encounter someone by a coffee machine, chat briefly after a meeting or conduct a telephone conversation. Informal though these encounters may be, you still may be coaching in various ways.

Action-focused coaching (AFC) focuses on an easy to recall structure of objectives, obstacles and action (see figure opposite). This structure is easy to recall and allows you to work through the issue systematically.

During the final action stage, you do not dictate the action. Instead, you encourage the person to discover for themselves the various possibilities, selecting the best course as they see it, not necessarily as you see it.

Listening

'Show me a coach, or a boss, who doesn't listen – really listen – and I'll show you a probable loser,' commented Brad Gilbert, the outstanding professional tennis player who became the top tennis coach of World Champions Andre Agassi and Andy Roddick. (See also Chapter 2.)

When coaching for results you pay close attention, showing you are alert by words and body language. You do not simply sit back and merely act like a sponge. If you are a specialist or expert in some area, you may be used to listening and then producing answers for people. Coaching does not work that way, since you avoid telling people what to do, instead helping them to discover the answers for themselves.

So, when acting as a coach avoid acting the know-it-all or responding with, 'Here's what I think you should do.' Instead, listen intently, then steer people towards finding the solution for themselves. Short term, this hands-off approach requires more time than giving them immediate answers. However, longer term, effective coaching encourages people to be self-reliant and therefore make fewer demands on you.

Limit your critical tendencies

Without looking, try chucking a tennis ball over your head behind you, making it drop into an empty waste bin a few feet away. Now imagine someone reporting on your efforts like this: 'That was absolutely terrible; you completely missed the bin, miles out!' Now, imagine doing it again, but this time the other person reports: 'You were six inches too far to the left and about a foot too long.' Which do you think is more help-ful to someone who wants to improve their performance at getting the ball in the bin?

curb any tendency to judge people

In management coaching, you may need to curb any tendency to judge people and instead give them an accuracy check. For example, is the person describing reality about their perfor-mance, are the facts correct, are they interpreting the situation positively or negatively?

Good management coaches ruthlessly separate facts from interpretation. Reflect back on what you think you have heard, and only then offer an interpretation.

Feedback

Feedback lies at the heart of coaching and leaves people feeling supported. To give useful feedback:

◆ acknowledge the person's feelings or viewpoint

◆ focus on potential improvements not mistakes

◆ stick to observable facts

◆ concentrate on required behaviours, not personality.

Great management coaches learn how to offer feedback in ways that the other person can accept. Sometimes this comes as engaging stories that inspire the other person to think differently about an issue, or it may happen through well-directed questions (see the section below). Alternatively, it may come in the form of helping the other person interpret evidence already in their possession: for example, 'You say people seldom really contribute much during your meetings. What do you think this is telling us about what is happening?'

Effective feedback works best when the other person feels ready to receive it. You need to work at preparing them to receive the information you wish to impart. For example, suppose you feel someone gives terrible presentations. While you could simply tell them your opinion, it may be far more effective to insist the person first conducts some personal enquiries into the effectiveness of their presentations. Having discovered there is considerable room for improvement, the person may then be more ready to receive your coaching on ways to improve their performance.

Questions

Helping someone discover ways to improve their performance will often depend on the questions you ask. Pose them in a spirit of curiosity and exploration, not as if conducting an inquisition into their behaviour.

Powerful coaching questions will have the following qualities.

◆ **Non-judgemental** – you do not infer a right or wrong answer, instead you leave the other with options to explore. *'How might you improve your presentation next time?'*

◆ **Simple and succinct** – you avoid complex questions suggesting you are an expert, instead you keep the questions short and simple, allowing the other person to start tackling them.
'What do you think is the main point of the presentation?'

◆ **Open** – these do not elicit a simple yes or no response since this kind of response will often stifle the coaching conversation abruptly.
'How can I help you?' or *'Tell me about your current role?'*

◆ **In tune with the other's thinking** – you choose a style of communication with which the other person can most easily connect.
'Do you feel good about that?'
'What do you think of that?'
'Is that what you hear from your colleagues?'

◆ **Reflective** – check your understanding and the underlying feelings.
'You seem to be angry about it, is that right?'

Challenge

Entire companies often respond well to what researcher and writer Jim Collins called Big Hairy and Audacious Goals. Equally, individuals may best improve their work performance through a coaching challenge. 'Treat people as if they are what they ought to be, and you help them become what they are capable of being,' argued the poet Goethe.

Before offering a coaching challenge, check first with your own internal coach. Are you doing it from a genuine desire to help the other person, or a wish to punish them in some way? If you feel a strong urge to tell the other person a few home truths, something you have wanted to do for a long time, then you are not in a coaching mode at all.

There are various ways to challenge without sounding as if you are out to 'get' the other person in some way. These include the following.

◆ **Confrontation** – rather than ignore difficult behaviour, instead you name it, explaining to the person what they are doing and why it is unacceptable.
'You keep interrupting people in meetings and it is making our meetings less enjoyable.'

◆ **Specific questions** – these challenge the person directly.
'Do you know why you get so angry when someone suggests you are wrong?'

◆ **State expectations** – say, clearly, what you want to happen.
'As we need you to work strictly within your budget next month, let's discuss how you can achieve that.'

◆ **Create boundaries** – people want to know what is acceptable at work, and your coaching session may need to set out the limits.
'It is hard to be constantly positive, but constant moaning in team meetings is not acceptable around here.'

In adopting a supporting, enabling style during coaching, there is always a danger of moving too far in this direction and losing sight of your essential managerial role. When the situation demands it, such as a mission-critical task, where failure would lead to disaster, you may need to demonstrate tough management. Here you show what you want and communicate clearly what you expect to change. (See also Chapter 13.)

Resistance

People will resist your coaching if they feel it will be punishing, concerned mainly with their faults, or an entirely one-sided conversation. Resistance also arises when someone feels,

'There's nothing wrong with me?' or asks, 'Why do I need any coaching?' This can be a delicate situation to resolve. An effective solution can be to separate initial problem description feedback strictly from any subsequent coaching sessions.

First, show convincingly why the person needs to change in some way, presenting them with clear factual evidence. For example:

◆ 'In your last three presentations the audience were unclear what your main point was. It seems you could benefit from some help on this issue.'

◆ 'This is the fourth time you have promised to deliver something on time but not met your commitment. We need to tackle this issue before it damages your career.'

Second, offer formal coaching only when the person agrees there is an issue to resolve.

Learning to coach

There are many workshops where you can safely practise coaching. During them, you will discover how to give feedback sensitively, influence with integrity, learn to trust your intuition and build the relationship.

Ways to coach for results

☐ *Make it a two-way affair in which you also develop*

☐ *Avoid telling people what to do, help them discover the answer*

☐ *Use the five-stage process: prepare, assess, explore, practise and review*

☐ *For quick coaching use objectives, obstacles and action*

☐ *Explore and learn to use known effective coaching techniques*

☐ *Listen actively*

☐ *Employ your intuition*

☐ *Ask questions in a positive way*

☐ *Influence with integrity*

☐ *Give feedback sensitively*

☐ *Show empathy despite setbacks*

☐ *Show compassion*

☐ *Work collaboratively*

☐ *Focus on action*

12

Negotiate successfully

IF YOU COULD QUIZ SHERLOCK HOLMES for the secret of his success, he would probably murmur, 'It's elementary.' The more obliging, equally fictitious detective Hercule Poirot might twiddle his gleaming black moustache and explain he spots and interprets clues that lesser mortals miss. Becoming a successful negotiator is like being a Sherlock Holmes or Hercule Poirot. You constantly search for clues to give your negotiations an edge. For behind the endless, deal-driven headlines, managers constantly negotiate. They bargain with customers and suppliers, with large shareholders, with potential alliance partners and with people inside their companies.

As Bob Davis, once CEO of the Spanish communications company Lycos put it: 'Companies have to make deal making a core competency.' You probably already know the basics of negotiating and may even be particularly good at it. Yet according to professor and negotiation expert James Sebenius, high stakes and intense pressure can cause costly mistakes. 'I'm struck by how frequently even experienced negotiators leave money on the table, deadlock, damage relationships or allow conflict to spiral.'

As a negotiation detective, be nosy. To understand the other side's problem, keep asking probing questions, and listen intently. And, like the TV sleuth Columbo, regardless of your outward manner, do it all from an inner confidence.

keep asking probing questions

Confidence at bargaining stems first from doing plenty of it. Secondly, it comes from knowing and using the learnable habits of effective negotiation, described below. Since most organisations regard highly those who can successfully negotiate, using these habits is an important way to thrive as a manager.

When it happens

Like a crime detective, you will encounter various types of cases. These include the following.

Informal occasions

> *'I want this report by Tuesday, how can we make that happen?'*
> *'If I chair the meeting, will you handle the time-keeping?'*

Informal bargaining occurs so often one hardly thinks twice about it. For instance, it is the start of informal negotiations if you ask your team to complete a job by midweek and they argue for doing it by the end of the week, or if you tell the boss you need a pay rise and only receive a non-committal response.

Formal negotiations

These may stem from informal ones. They involve bosses, trade unions and other bodies and can be over wages, working arrangements or some area of activity.

> *'If we provide you with the full data, would you hold off action until next month?'*

'We need more flexibility in overtime working; will your members accept that in exchange for a guarantee of a minimum amount monthly?'

Negotiations with a trade union or other representative bodies will seldom be informal, except perhaps early on. Usually these encounters become like a carefully choreographed dance, with everyone knowing the right moves.

Commercial bargaining

This aims to achieve a business deal, for example a new contract with a supplier, a merger arrangement, tackling the terms of a sale.

'At what price would you consider committing to a five-year contract with us?'
'Our cancellation arrangements differ from your proposed procurement contract; can we explore how to resolve this?'

Negotiations fail for as many reasons as there are individuals and deals. Yet there are several common mistakes which, with care, you can certainly avoid.

Most negotiations are like a six-act stage play. The curtain goes up after lots of rehearsals – that is, intense preparations. Then the first actors appear, setting the scene and, in negotiation terms, making the initial offer. The real show begins when the actors strut their stuff, which in negotiation terms is about clarifying the situation so everyone knows what is going on. As each scene unfolds, we usually see lots of interaction – the bargaining stage. The curtain comes down with some kind of resolution – the close of the negotiation. Once the performance ends, the cast continues making improvements, which in negotiation terms is follow-through or implementation.

Classic negotiation mistakes

◆ **Don't bother understanding the other side's problem.** You can only negotiate effectively if you understand both your own interests and those of your counterpart. You need to address these as a way of solving your own problem.

◆ **Make price dominate everything.** If you focus exclusively on price you turn potentially cooperative deals into adversarial ones. This is a common mistake of inexperienced managers fixated on creating win/lose outcomes.

◆ **Neglect the best alternative.** You may be better off with no deal at all. It may be better to walk away, prolong a stalemate, make something in-house instead, procure a product externally, or write it off.

◆ **Skewed vision.** You may feel you see the negotiation situation clearly, yet like a pilot's sense of the horizon at night, it can be wildly wrong. Misreading the situation leads to negotiation errors.

These six scenes – prepare, offer, clarify, bargain, close and implement – may blur at the edges, occurring quickly without gaps between them. But make sure you keep track of where you are in the entire negotiation.

Invest in preparation

Golfing legend Gary Player once explained: 'The more I practise, the luckier I get.' Several millennia earlier Sun Tzu, writing about the art of warfare, put it slightly differently: 'Every battle is won before it is ever fought.'

Research into negotiation usually focuses on the cut and thrust of actual deal making. Yet no matter how many right moves you make, or however skilled you become at reading body language, building trust, framing arguments, or making offers or counter-offers, success ultimately stems from good preparation. Careful preparation ensures you take the steps you need to be at the right table at the right time, with the right people and in possession of the right information. Far too many managers fondly believe they are great negotiators and enter these situations woefully underprepared.

Curiously, skilled and average negotiators tend to prepare for roughly the same amount of time. The difference lies in how each uses time. Average performers spend most of their preparation gathering data and massaging the numbers. In contrast, skilled negotiators devote most of their time to detective work, exploring soft issues and strategy, and deducing what the numbers tell them.

Good preparation means defining the answers to questions such as:

◆ What do we want from this negotiation?

◆ What would be our ideal outcome?

◆ What would be an acceptable outcome?

◆ What is an unacceptable result – when would we walk away?

◆ What are our negotiating strengths and weaknesses and what are theirs?

In high-stakes poker, the top professionals like to look as if they have just turned up. In fact, the best of them prepare meticulously for the event. Entering management negotiation with the above issues clear in your mind allows you to arrive at the table, like a professional poker player, with confidence and in possession of important knowledge.

What do successful negotiators need?

◆ A quick mind

◆ A strong reserve of patience

◆ The capacity to conceal without lying

◆ To inspire trust

◆ To realise when to be assertive and when to be self-effacing

◆ Knowledge of the issue

◆ The ability to see the bigger picture

◆ To ask plenty of questions

◆ To stick to one of two strong arguments, not many supporting ones

To experience the full horrors of inadequate preparation, try negotiating with a skilled trade unionist. They usually receive in-depth training and if you find yourself in this territory, it could be well worth investing in some suitable off-site learning for yourself.

try negotiating with a skilled trade unionist

Assess your bargaining power

There was little room to negotiate with Mongol chieftain Genghis Khan. It got nasty and violent if you tried. When most of the power resides with the other side, there is little scope to bargain. Solving the mystery of how much bargaining power you possess may require all your detection skills, and be a critical factor in achieving a successful deal.

Experienced negotiators also constantly seek ways to strengthen their bargaining power or to weaken that of the other party. Naturally, your bargaining power influences the kind of outcome you can expect:

◆ win/lose – you gain but the other party loses

◆ win/win – you both gain a mutual benefit

◆ lose/lose – neither party gains a benefit.

These all assume the result is like a cake, fixed in size. Negotiation comes down to fighting for one's rightful share. Nowadays though, a more sophisticated approach assumes the cake can be both expanded and divided.

Game theory, which uses advanced maths, can sometimes help with the detective work of assessing power and potential outcomes by providing insight into how rational people behave when negotiating. However, newer approaches no longer assume rational behaviour.

Despite all the complexity of outcomes available, the best negotiators are those who prefer using their power to achieve a result that leaves everyone feeling good about it.

Adopt successful habits

What skilled negotiators do more of	What skilled negotiators do less of
◆ Check they have understood the other side – 'Let's recap on where we are.'	◆ Give information – 'Did you know...?'
◆ Ask for reasons – 'Can you justify that?'	◆ Acknowledge the person or their point – 'Yes quite, but as I was saying...'
◆ Ask for terms – 'What would your ideal volume be?'	◆ Disagree or contradict – 'No, but...'
◆ Create doubt – 'Have you considered the implications for...?'	◆ Make assumptions – 'I take it then that...'

Habit 1

Always know at what point you would be willing to walk away from the table. With this clear in your mind, you will feel a natural confidence about bargaining.

Habit 2

Be sure to include your highest value player. You cannot negotiate well in the absence of the person, organisation or representative who would get the best from the deal.

Habit 3

Include the most influential players who can make a difference to whether the negotiation succeeds or fails. This is more than demanding to see the organ grinder rather than the monkey. Look carefully to identify whom you most need around the table from the other side, to give the best chance of success.

Habit 4

Set up the right no-deal situation. It may pay you to bring in other parties to bolster your no-deal option. For example, transforming a two-party discussion into more of an auction can change the psychology of the deal, as well as the competitive pressures.

Habit 5

Where you want someone else to negotiate on your behalf, make sure they have the right skills to win the best deal. For example, will the agent really bargain hard enough for you?

Habit 6

Keep it simple and minimise the number of different parties involved. Too many people can complicate a negotiation, making it unwieldy.

Habit 7

Keep asking 'Why?' Do not merely discuss what your counter-part wants, uncover *why* they want it. Skilled negotiators are question addicts, asking more than twice as many questions as less skilled ones ask.

Use persistence

Top negotiators may claim their success relies on one key reason. It could be their willingness to walk away from a deal, knowing exactly what they want, good preparation and so on. One sure-fire guideline and the title of an excellent book by Gavin Kennedy is *Everything is Negotiable*.

While there are some situations where no negotiations seem possible, these are rare. For example, the widely made claim that 'we won't talk to terrorists' often proves to be spurious. In search of a political solution in Northern Ireland, the Blair government secretly offered to meet masked IRA representatives, despite repeated claims to the contrary.

Having tried to close a deal and been rejected, is it the end of the road? Not necessarily. It may be that it is worth continuing to play detective, investigating possible solutions and a powerful question to pursue is: 'What will it take to reach an agreement, despite our present difficulties?'

Following a no-deal response, it may seem costly to continue negotiating. But if you are confused about *why* your deal fell apart, it could be even more expensive to abandon it. Instead, next time you apparently lose a deal and head for the door, stick around and continue playing detective. What you discover may prove surprising, and allow you to put the deal back on track.

Specialist negotiators

Working in the HR department of a large company, Brian Jones (not his real name) decided to use Maynard Leigh Associates to deliver a culture change programme. Under his company rules though, the detailed contractual arrangements became the responsibility of the procurement department. The in-house negotiations experts started playing hardball, exerting sustained pressure on Maynard Leigh over price and cancellation terms. Eventually the Maynard Leigh consultant complained to Brian of bullying. Brian who did not want to drive away his preferred supplier, found himself negotiating with the procurement department to adjust its approach to the deal.

Companies often rely on specialist negotiators, like procurement officers, to extract the best bargains. The rise of these experts reflects the realisation that poor negotiating by line managers may leave an organisation exposed to both wasteful costs and avoidable risks. However, even if you succeed in delegating the bargaining job, you will seldom escape becoming involved in the issues associated with it. Make sure those who bargain on your behalf have both the skills and your interests at heart to do the best deal.

companies often rely on specialist negotiators to extract the best bargains

---

Ways to negotiate successfully

☐ *Infuse your negotiations with patience combined with persistence*

☐ *Do your homework thoroughly on the negotiation issue*

☐ *Use the six stages of negotiation (prepare, offer, clarify, bargain, close and implement) to enhance your preparations for a deal*

☐ Research the position of the other party to uncover what they most want

☐ Establish:
  – ideal outcome
  – acceptable outcome
  – when you would definitely walk away from the negotiations
  – what is negotiable
  – what is non-negotiable

☐ Keep returning to the bigger picture into which your negotiations fit

☐ Use varied questions to shed light on the position of the other party

☐ Rely on one or two strong arguments to support your position, rather than many

☐ Even if eventually you cannot achieve it, aim for a win/win situation

☐ Keep searching for common ground as a route to a deal

☐ Explore the alternatives to doing a deal

13

Handle problem people

'TWO MOANS AND YOU'RE OUT' became the policy at IT specialist Nutzwerk after a successful anti-moaning campaign. 'If you are negative at Eden, you are fired,' CEO and co-founder of the Eden Project, Tim Smit says. 'Negative people are a cancer in the creative workplace.' Moaners can indeed be toxic and are just some of the types of problem people you may encounter and need to manage.

What seems a problem person though, may only be someone making your life difficult, for instance, by challenging your judgements, questioning your decisions, continually demanding explanations. Such behaviour may be awkward, yet may also be productive.

It can be dangerous branding someone as a problem person. First, they may just be different. Every organisation needs its mavericks. These people think counterintuitively, seeing the world in unexpected ways. Despite their problematic behaviour, they can be a vital source of new ideas, defining the future or solving previously intractable problems. Secondly, problem people may be good at their job, despite their unwanted behaviour. They may simply have temporary difficulties and need your support, not punishment or the sack. Thirdly, by

every organisation needs its mavericks

naming someone a problem person you potentially create a scapegoat who becomes an unwilling magnet for all kinds of blame. Not only may this be unfair, it may eventually lead to an expensive claim for discrimination damages.

No one comes to work in order to fail. Start by assuming you have no problem people, only ones with problems, being in the wrong job, managed incorrectly or facing temporary difficulties. This is your chance to show you can get the best from people.

Even experienced managers sometimes admit, 'I've run out of ideas on how to deal with him,' or, 'She could do so much better but nothing seems to work,' or 'He simply can't follow instructions.' Many feel stressed over dealing with their difficult people.

Since under the right circumstances problem people can often be highly effective, try viewing their behaviour not as a problem but as a symptom. You need to alter behaviour, not their personality.

Confronted about their problem employees, senior managers sometimes confess the issue has been around for years. They simply never got round to resolving it. By tolerating poor behaviour and underperformance, you make it harder to manage the rest of your people who naturally draw conclusions about the acceptance of adverse behaviour. Rather than allow adverse behaviour to drift on for weeks or even months, take action. (See Chapter 10.)

Problem people

◆ Low fliers – sloppy or slow workers;
   procrastinators; latecomers.

◆ Power players – abrasive toughies, or people who are
   insensitive, loud or confrontational; prima donnas who
   throw a tantrum until they get what they want.

◆ Whiners* – moaners who are perpetually finding fault;
pessimists with hundreds of reasons why things can't be
done; 'victims', who complain of unfair treatment.

◆ Deceivers – political players; those who manoeuvre around
the rules; gossips who spread misrepresentations; resisters
with out-of-control habits such as drinking.

◆ Bullies – these get what they want through using excessive
confrontation, conflict and a disregard for the views and
feelings of others.

◆ Liars – these distort information, manipulate and leave a trail
of distrust and, for example, undermine effective teamwork.

◆ Worriers – overanxious individuals who instead of turning
their anxieties into useful behaviour, such as attention to
detail, demand constant attention and reassurance.

*HR experts say these are the hardest to deal with.

Put it in perspective

Inexperienced managers or ones with a short fuse may rapidly
conclude someone is a problem person and demand: 'I want
them off the bus – now!' This may be a sensible decision, but
start by assuming the person needs support, not punishment.
Before concluding you really have a problem person on your
hands, raise your awareness about the nature of the behaviour.
For example, how serious, frequent or entrenched is the behaviour, and what is the overall context of the problem? Only
through awareness can you expect to develop your insight to
arrive at practical solutions.

How serious?

Being around annoying, irritating or distracting people can be a pain. Yet how damaging is their behaviour? Does it affect other people's performance? Are they undermining your reputation or the team's? Do they lose the company money, customers or customers' respect? Put their actions in a larger perspective and decide whether it warrants any action at all.

How frequent?

Binge drinking twice a week may start to affect someone's work performance or endanger their health. If it occurs once a year celebrating a team success, it hardly warrants remedial action. Examine the facts about frequency. With a high-performer for instance, it may not be worth devoting time and energy to tackling occasional lapses.

How deeply entrenched?

You do not have time to tackle deep-seated behavioural problems, such as phobias or other forms of psychological disturbance. You may only be able to discover whether behaviour is deeply entrenched by holding one or more performance review sessions. (See Chapter 10.) If necessary, refer the person to other experts, such as therapists or specialist coaches.

Do we fully understand the context of this problem?

Make or obtain a detailed description of where the adverse behaviour happens and under what circumstances. When you come to examine the facts, you may conclude the person is reacting to particular kinds of situations where they feel under threat, out of their depth, or in response to excessive demands made on them.

Major change programmes, for instance, can unsettle people so much that they start showing resistance or behaving in unexpected ways. These symptoms may fade away once the change effort has taken hold.

Define it

Describe adverse behaviour with actual examples. It is not enough to know someone constantly arrives late to meetings. Back it up with dates, times and places. Solid facts about a problem help you become clearer about suitable action. For example, is the cause internal to the person or external?

◆ **Internal factors** – these are internal to the person such as poor motivation, hates meetings, poor time-keeping, low morale, bored, low drive, lacks ideas, impatient, poor concentration.

◆ **External factors** – these impinge on the person, such as over-long meetings, tired from overwork, seldom asked for an opinion, excessive workload, unwell, long commute, family problems, being bullied, suffering prejudice or discrimination.

By separating out and identifying these two factors, you will be a long way towards knowing how best to help this employee change.

Modifying behaviour

You do not need to be a therapist or brain surgeon to alter someone's problem behaviour. There is a whole kit bag of tools for tackling adverse behaviour, including counselling, performance reviews, training, confrontation, job restructuring, transfers, punishment and dismissal.

there is a whole kit bag of tools for tackling adverse behaviour

One of the most effective managerial tools is behaviour modification (BM), which has nothing to do with brainwashing or other dubious practices. BM influences people's behaviour using ideas from psychological research and practical experience. Using it, you ignore possible causes, focusing instead on direct action to influence behaviour. It aims to:

◆ affect the triggers that set off someone's behaviour, or

◆ reward the results of positive behaviours.

If you can discover what sets off someone's adverse behaviour you can try to alter or eliminate this factor. For instance, by continually warning someone to produce their reports on time you may merely be triggering their resistance to delivering in the first place. Rewarding is the second way to alter behaviour. For example, a team member may constantly interrupt because they realise it gains them attention. Or they learn through experience that it pays to use rudeness to avoid some task or responsibility.

Change the reward they get from their adverse behaviour and you begin affecting their actions. Rewards come in many guises, so do not think solely in terms of money. Praise, for instance, can be far more important. Punishment, a negative form of reward, can also affect behaviour. However, it tends to have unpredictable consequences and usually proves to be a poor way to manage. You quickly run out of options by relying on punishment to try to alter behaviour.

Reinforcement

Catch them doing something right and reward it. This long-standing BM approach helps you strengthen behaviour in the right direction and weaken adverse behaviours. For example, if you smile each time someone you manage says 'good morning' you will be positively reinforcing this behaviour and they are likely to repeat it. Similarly, by constantly tolerating persistent lateness in meetings and welcoming latecomers with a full summary of what has happened so far, you reinforce their adverse behaviour and they have every reason to continue it.

Reinforcement works best through encouraging small steps towards the final behaviour you want. You do not necessarily shoot for the moon immediately. Instead, you look for signs, no matter how small, that someone is changing in the right direction and reinforce these.

Suppose someone repeatedly delivers work several days late. After drawing attention to this and making sure there are no external factors to consider, you ask for an improvement. If the person delivers their work only slightly late next time, you reinforce this with encouragement, not another complaint. You might say for instance: *'Well done, I know this must have been quite an effort and I really appreciate how hard you have tried to deliver it on time. This really helps me with my own deadlines.'*

Modifying behaviour

Step 1: Decide what the new behaviour needs to be: for example, arrives on time for team meetings and fully prepared.

Step 2: Break down the change needed into smaller behavioural changes needed to reach the overall change. For example:

◆ still arrives late but much less than last time

◆ arrives hardly late but still unprepared

◆ arrives on time but still unprepared

◆ arrives on time and shows signs of doing some preparation

◆ arrives early and is fully prepared.

Step 3:   Watch for *any* behaviour moving in the direction of the first new behaviour. No matter how tentative the sign, describe it to the person, and offer support, encouragement and recognition; explain how it helps, for example, *'When you clearly try to arrive on time, this really helps the team meeting get off to a good start.'*

Step 4:   Continue reinforcing the new behaviour; that is, encouraging or rewarding, whenever the behaviour occurs until it seems permanent.

Step 5:   Now watch for any signs that behaviour is moving in the desired direction of the next step and reinforce/reward.

Confrontation

In tackling the problem person are you worried about making an unpleasant scene? Would you rather do almost anything to avoid such a scene? Even experienced managers sometimes duck a confrontation for fear of damaging a relationship or being unable to handle a colleague becoming emotional. Yet confrontation need not always be a miserable experience; it can be satisfying and inspiring. With confrontation you tackle adverse behaviour as it occurs or shortly afterwards. For example, you might establish a team rule that if someone behaves badly you will treat it like a speeding fine, tackling it within two weeks or not at all.

Promptness prevents resentment building to undermine respect and trust. Before it becomes deep-rooted, use regular development sessions to confront and uncover potentially troublesome behaviour. For example, you might ask team members to sit opposite each other in pairs and in five minutes discuss:

◆ 'What I really appreciate about you is...'

◆ 'What I want less of from you is....'

'I' statements

Although being a manager means you constantly use 'we' rather than 'I', when you confront someone over their problem behaviour it is usually best to use an 'I' statement, which makes it clear you are speaking for yourself, rather than other people. This makes the issue more real for the other person:

◆ *'I want you to pay attention during our meetings when someone else has the floor and is talking.'*

◆ *'I need this room to be really tidy by the time the MD arrives tomorrow.'*

Avoid indirect statements such as 'the team feels...', 'the company would like...' or 'it's not the done thing round here'. Positive confrontation consists of saying what you want, rather than what you do *not* want:

◆ rather than: *'Please stop talking to colleagues while I am briefing the team'*

◆ use instead: *'I want your full attention while I am briefing the team'*.

Confrontation often works best when based on careful preparation, rather than plunging in immediately without marshalling the evidence or planning your strategy.

Common sense tells you to stay calm and not lose your temper with the problem person, but this hardly helps in knowing how to tackle the situation. Rather than confront on the spot when the adverse behaviour

it may be better to hold back

occurs, it may be better to hold back and arrange the encounter for a time of your own choosing.

Managing a confrontation

In response to a disruptive team member:

◆ Gather evidence about how the rest of the team feels about the behaviour.

◆ Invite the person concerned to meet you in your office, in private.

◆ Describe the adverse effects of their behaviour on colleagues. Do not use 'team members feel this or that...' but practical examples, with your conclusions about the effects:

– 'I notice you keep interrupting at team meetings, and I see some members feeling angry with you.'

– 'When you rudely criticised Peter in the meeting not only did it upset him but it affected others in that way too.'

◆ Ask them to explain why they behave in this way.

◆ Invite them to behave differently next time.

◆ Explore ways in which they might alter their behaviour in the future. For example, 'Try using your sense of humour to see the funny side of someone being stupid in the meeting.'

Mediation

Mediation can resolve many difficult workplace conflicts between people and some managers become highly skilled at it. It helps create more adult-to-adult relationships in all areas of work. Royal Mail, for example, uses a mix of internal and external mediators.

A core part of the mediation skill is awareness that a conflict exists and would benefit from mediation. This might take the form of helping the people concerned tell others how they feel about some disagreement or situation. As you need confidence to handle a mediation situation it may be worth seeking some training in this area.

Sack 'em!

This is the nuclear option and many would argue a sign of ultimate managerial failure. Dismissal is seldom a pleasant task, even when the person has been troublesome for a long time. Also, employment legislation makes it essential to avoid this option if possible. At some point in your management career though, you will be stuck with a problem person whose behaviour seems unmanageable. If you decide on dismissal, seek professional advice on how best to go about this since it is difficult terrain and can be costly if handled badly.

It is essential to reduce the possibility of legal action with sound documentation, such as up-to-date recorded warnings, and specific failures to perform described in terms of time and place. Dismissal can be a lengthy process, particularly in large organisations where advisers such as HR specialists and lawyers ensure you have jumped through all the right hoops in sequence.

Finally, do not take the process to heart. While it is no minor matter to sack someone, it does not have to be personally destructive for you either.

Ways to deal with problem people

☐ *Take control of the situation, not the person*

☐ *Head off trouble before it can turn into a disaster*

☐ *Learn to read behaviour, so you can objectively describe what is happening*

☐ *Separate internal factors causing behaviour problems from external ones*

☐ *Aim to leave the person feeling you want to help them, not punish or reprimand them*

☐ *Avoid using attitude as your definition of the problem*

☐ *Get beyond the label to more objective factors such as rudeness, lateness, lack of professionalism or failure to cooperate*

☐ *Consider how frequent, serious and entrenched their adverse behaviour is – is it worth tackling?*

☐ *Aim to alter behaviour, not their personality*

☐ *Confront seriously adverse behaviour immediately, do not let things drift*

☐ *Understand the context, not just the personality*

☐ *Effective confrontation starts with an 'I' statement about what you want*

☐ *Seek professional advice if you go for dismissal*

PART 3

Manage the organisation

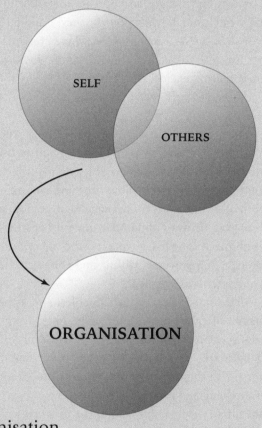

Organisation

◆ Manage change
◆ Make decisions
◆ Inspire meetings
◆ Encourage creativity and innovation
◆ Select and recruit
◆ Show integrity
◆ Encourage diversity

Managing the organisation is being aware of the situation, realising the impact you want to make or could make, and how to make it. The seven management processes require you to hone your awareness and insight so you can affect not just those you manage but a much wider constituency. Can you imagine working in a commercial organisation where everyone around you is a volunteer? To get anything done you would probably have to negotiate, persuade, wheel and deal. At any time, your army of volunteers could instantly choose to direct their energies elsewhere.

This is not quite the bizarre scenario it seems. Knowledge workers are now central to how many organisations operate and they do not take kindly to old-style management and leadership based on hierarchy, low trust and control. As Gary Hamel, international guru on management argues, such old ways of making things happen 'sit uneasily against a paradigm of volunteer knowledge workers who are expected to be accountable and empowered, willing and able to create shared learning and intellectual capital'.

If the environment proves unpalatable many experts and specialists can literally vote with their feet. Indeed entire teams of financial specialists, for example, regularly jump ship when tempted by better conditions or other inducements. Your interactions with the organisation are therefore an important aspect of surviving and thriving as a manager.

This third part deals with seven of the most critical aspects of managing the organisation: manage time and goals, manage change, make decisions, inspire meetings, encourage creativity and innovation, select and recruit, and finally persuade and influence.

14

Manage change

HAVE YOU EVER BEEN WHITE WATER RAFTING? If not, you have probably caught TV scenes of helmeted thrill-seekers battling the currents, steering their vulnerable craft over rapids and away from dangerous rocks and reefs. Managing change in organisations is rather like that. Once you become a manager, you automatically join the boat crew, and may even sometimes be the captain. With change pervasive and constantly accelerating, you could just sit back in your office and let nature take its course. But as with white water rafting, even when the currents seem benign, it seldom makes sense to abandon your fate to them.

Successful managers become change agents. They learn to deal with it even if, like the white water rafter, they cannot entirely control either the speed or direction of the journey. Going with the flow may seem an easy option, yet can make you entirely reactive, so you feel out of control of the swirling changes happening around you.

Being a change agent mainly concerns tackling organisational shifts, rather than altering a specific person's behaviours. At a personal level, it challenges you to live with uncertainty, tolerate ambiguity and avoid becoming

avoid becoming dangerously risk averse

dangerously risk averse. Managing change is tough and studies show that in most organisations two out of three attempts fail. The more things change the more they stay the same.

The organic view

In an ant colony, there is no boss sending out orders, yet important decisions still emerge. A river never agonises about where to flow, yet still the water finds its own level. These are complex adaptive systems, offering important lessons for anyone attempting to create change in a human organisation.

Like the ant colony or a river, companies and people are also complex adaptive systems. That is, even with intensive study they are largely unpredictable. Simple rules of cause and effect do not necessarily apply. Foreseeing the outcome from a particular change will nearly always be hit and miss.

This organic view differs from treating the organisation as a machine, where pulling a particular lever will produce a known effect. An organic approach to change may seem wildly removed from the world of management. Yet taking it can prevent you from making wrong assumptions or having unreal expectations about likely results of change programmes. For example, an organic approach to change means accepting that there will be uncertain results from most important decisions. Even so, the right choices will often emerge naturally.

Rather than relying on so-called rational decision making, with the organic perspective you allow creative solutions to surface naturally. With this approach, you steer change, rather than direct it.

Route maps

'You have reached your destination,' drones the robotic, schoolmistress voice of the on-board SatNav. It would be wonderful if these ubiquitous devices could also tell us how to reach our chosen destination regarding organisational change. Unfortunately, no one has yet invented a credible SatNav for organisational change, and there are over 6000 books on change and management, each with their own take on how best to do it.

Without a reliable SatNav for organisational change, you will need to evolve your own route map of how best to make it happen. The four signposts to plant along your way are as follows.

1 Treat change as a process, not as a one-off, single event.

2 Assess carefully how long the change will take to complete.

3 Be clear how many people will be needed to execute the change.

4 Clarify the financial benefits and cost of the proposed change.

Treating organisational change as a continuous process means you act more like someone at the tiller of a sailing boat, constantly making small adjustments and the occasional large one, than someone pressing a button.

Operational versus strategic

As a change agent, it helps if you distinguish between operational change and fundamental strategic change.

- ◆ **Operational change** consists of alterations in procedures or activities. Because these mainly deal with day-to-day matters, you give less attention to exploring or anticipating long-term implications.

- ◆ **Strategic change** deals with cultural, structural, market or process shifts. These will tend to have long-term implications for how the organisation functions and require both careful thought and detailed planning.

Apart from using this distinction, what else might appear on your mental route map of achieving organisational change? It might include these specific activities:

◆ develop a change strategy – setting out how you will get there

◆ use vision and values – applying 'big picture' thinking to where you want to go

◆ use personal leadership – showing people how to get there

◆ deal with conflict and resistance – overcoming blockages to change

◆ encourage fresh thinking – generating new perspectives about change

◆ obtain commitment – engaging people's enthusiasm and energy

◆ adopt project management – instilling ways to progress and monitoring the change process

◆ communicate – making sure all stakeholders know what they need to know

◆ make change stick – embedding the changes so old ways do not return.

Develop a change strategy

The simplest route map for organisational change explains your expected destination. It is a move from

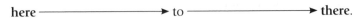

here ⟶ to ⟶ **there**.

This may sound dangerously naive, yet more change efforts fail from lack of clarity about the intended destination than practically any other cause. (See also Chapter 3.)

By treating the planned change as a journey, not a destination, you will almost naturally tend to break it into stages, without necessarily assuming there is an end.

Use vision and values

How did the struggling Co-operative bank of the 1990s become a more vibrant and effective organisation, well positioned to succeed in the 21st century? Likewise, how did M&S, seemingly destined to fall into the maw of hungry predators, bounce back? Both organisations experienced a successful transformation. The Co-operative bank did it by building on its core values to create a modern and vibrant new culture. M&S returned to its core values of style and value for money, while shaking up a moribund organisation.

Values tell people how you want things to be – that is, what matters. They bind a team or an entire company together like a glue to give change programmes coherence. Talk, talk, talk the values! Your job as a change agent is first to articulate values, secondly to explain how to turn them into practical action, and finally to demonstrate them by your own behaviour. When you model the way, others will follow.

talk, talk, talk the values!

Apply personal leadership

As explained in Chapter 7, effective managers show leadership. In managing change, this means you step out there and describe the desired future. People need to see you thinking and acting strategically.

So, what are your organisation's aspirations and strategic intent? If you do not know, find out, even if this appears to be notionally outside your immediate area of responsibility. Do this by seeking answers to questions like:

◆ Where is this organisation going?

◆ Where can it or should it go?

◆ What are we ultimately trying to achieve (avoid simplistic answers like 'to make a profit' or 'world domination')?

◆ What is our corporate vision for the future?

Not all senior colleagues may welcome your enquiries, particularly if they themselves feel unsure of the answers. When people see you ask the questions though, it will certainly raise your profile, so long as you do it from a genuine sense of curiosity.

Handle conflict and resistance

'Resistance is futile' goes the famous line from the sinister Borg in the TV series *Star Trek*. Not only is resistance to change often not futile, it may be entirely rational. When Shell met strong staff reaction to dumping one of its oil rigs in the North Sea, the internal staff anger was entirely appropriate. Had the company leadership listened better, it would have avoided the damaging public reaction, which later forced a painful reversal.

Resistance to a change may conveniently happen in a low-key way. Equally, it may erupt into conflict, pitting one group against another, producing damaging splits across the organisation. Conflict invariably involves emotion and strong feelings. Consequently, conflict management is unavoidably part of the basic skills of any manager who aspires to be a successful change agent.

Practical actions include:

◆ bringing conflict to the surface rather than allowing it to fester

◆ working with those experiencing it to dissect and analyse what it is really about

◆ treating conflict as usually healthy, adding rigour to decisions

◆ acting as a mediator, nudging the parties to get closer or compromise

◆ controlling the escalation of tension by thinking ahead and nipping issues in the bud.

Are you comfortable with such a situation, or do you fervently wish to be anywhere else than in the eye of the storm? Consider using an external resource such as a specialist workshop on conflict resolution to boost your skills and confidence in this area.

Manage risk

From mastering the deadly sabretoothed tiger to facing up to climate change, human survival has always depended on dealing with risk. In fact, risk avoidance is a natural human instinct. Any organisational change effort you are involved in will come with some kind of risk attached to it. Part of your role as change agent will be making sense of the nature and extent of that risk.

If you manage IT systems, risk assessment is almost a profession in its own right. In organisational change, though, calculation of risk is nowhere near that level of sophistication. Therefore, what matters most is ensuring risk does not turn into recklessness. Reckless organisational change occurs when managers make unreasonable assumptions about the likely benefits or outcomes from a particular change initiative.

At the macro level, the poor record of success in mergers and acquisitions with few delivering their expected business benefits shows how risk can become reckless, destroying shareholder value and achieving little practical benefit for years to come. At the micro level, even minor structural changes, such as who reports to whom or how certain types of projects will be handled, can trigger all kinds of unexpected and sometimes destructive forces.

Assess the risks and, where possible, quantify them.

Obtain commitment

'It is a marathon, not a sprint,' say those familiar with organisational change efforts. Large-scale change seldom proves simple or quick. Effective change agents know their biggest challenge in new ways of working, behaving or thinking is winning people's commitment.

For the changes you want to make you will need to seek visible backing from the most influential people in your organisation, who may not necessarily hold the top titles. You also need to take into account the enthusiasm, or lack of it, of those who will deal with the new systems, processes or ways of working.

Who are the stakeholders affected by the change you have in mind? How will you gain their involvement? Stakeholders who will support or oppose the change will implicitly be asking, 'What's in it for me?' There is nothing particularly selfish or self-serving about this response. People only absorb the case for change by personalising it, relating it to themselves, to their own job, their team or even their family.

Decide whom you need to commit to the change, and how to involve them in the whole process.

Adopt project management

The soft side of change management gets plenty of attention. But the hard side matters too, focusing on detailed implementation and breaking the change effort into manageable projects.

Your project teams need clear goals with recognisable milestones, with regular reporting on progress. They also need to accept that anyone not directly involved in the change work has scope to increase their workload in the change cause by probably not more than 10 per cent. More than this and people will become overstretched and unable to support the change initiative.

Choose your project leaders for their enthusiasm for the change effort, not just because they are good technicians or competent professionals.

choose your project leaders for their enthusiasm

Communicate

'It's good to talk' went a famous BT advertising slogan and much the same applies to change programmes. Many start with a solid communication effort to explain what will happen and when. But far too many such efforts are more like product branding exercises than a continuous conversation between people. Without a continuous dialogue between those seeking change and those who must make it happen, people can soon feel out of touch. They wonder, for example, if the change effort is failing, or they lose the motivation to stay involved.

Build a continuous communications process into your change strategy. It may take varied forms, from regular town hall meetings to monthly newsletters, from e-mail updates to celebrations of reaching critical stages in the programme.

Be proactive in personally talking about the change programme, making yourself available to people who have concerns about it, or are responsible for some aspect of implementation. Find imaginative ways to remind staff of the overall case for change and to reinforce its benefits to them.

Make change stick

Any fool can launch a change programme. To make it stick though, demands a combination of awareness, insight and persistence. You need to become constantly aware of where you are in the programme and be ready to take action against inertia and a natural tendency to return to old patterns of behaviour.

Vary the ways you keep the momentum going. Your persistence agenda might include: publicity to reinforce the basic change message constantly; talks by change enthusiasts; celebrations; clever use of procedures and policies; small interactions over coffee or by the water cooler; mass e-mails; write-ups in the media or internal newsletters; and town hall type meetings.

you need to find champions for your change effort

Because most change efforts are a journey not a destination, you need to find champions for your change effort. Their job is to keep raising the profile of the programme by talking about it, encouraging action and using their influence to make an impact.

Ways to manage change

☐ *Develop your ability to tolerate ambiguity and uncertainty*

☐ *View your organisation as more like a living organism than a machine*

☐ *Master the differences between operational and strategic change*

☐ *Start to develop your own route map for managing the organisation's change*

☐ *View change efforts as a journey, not a destination*

☐ Articulate values and explain how they will be turned into practical action

☐ Demonstrate change values through your own behaviour

☐ Build an engaging word picture of how the future should look

☐ Talk constantly about the change programme and show your enthusiasm for it

☐ Develop your capacity to think and act strategically

☐ Anticipate resistance to change with strategies for dealing with it

☐ Treat conflict as healthy, adding rigour to change decisions

☐ Practise thinking outside the box and encouraging others to do the same

☐ Identify who are the stakeholders affected by the change

☐ Discover the best people to be involved in implementation

☐ Break down the overall change into small, more manageable chunks

☐ Use project teams to tackle chunks of the change effort

☐ Build a continuous communications process into your change strategy

☐ Establish regular monitoring systems to tell you what is happening

☐ Make change stick using persistence and by enrolling champions to promote it

15

Make decisions

ASKED HOW SHE HAD MANAGED TO SUCCEED in such a male-dominated environment, the first woman admiral in America, the formidable Grace Hopper, reportedly growled her secret for successful decision making: 'I guess you do it first, and apologise later.'

The detached and impassive executive may fit our mental picture of the ideal corporate decision maker, yet people actually make better choices when they experience intense emotions. Ignoring the emotional content of a decision can also prove costly.

British Airways changed the design of all its aircraft tail fins by dropping the Union Flag in favour of art from around the world. The company based its expensive repainting decision almost entirely on the numbers from consumer feedback. But a smaller group of highly-profitable and influential customers, who disliked the new design, eventually forced the airline to scrap it. The best decision makers embrace emotions and the use of intuition, without allowing these to lead them astray.

making decisions is what managers are supposed to do

Making decisions is what managers are supposed to do. Real life can be very different. The number of decisions made by a new or relatively inexperienced manager is far less than the traditional image of a busy manager. So it is important that the ones you do make are as good as they can be.

Only robots make decisions based entirely on numerical data. But a whole science of decision making uses complex models, subtle theories and clever systems for identifying options, attaching probabilities and assessing risk. Is that what the management job is really about, and does it mean you must master this discipline or risk being a failure?

'Often you have to rely on your intuition,' remarked Microsoft's Bill Gates. This gets you closer to how the world actually works.

Satisficing

In studying those making high-stake choices, researchers initially assumed they would be rational, just like the decision models predict:

> *Gather information, identify possible solutions, choose the best ones, and evaluate the results.*

Their assumptions were wrong.

The evidence revealed people seldom bother with comparing difference choices. Instead, they merely find something better than their starting point. They commonly select *the first reasonable option they encounter* – an approach called satisficing. It happens because of time pressures, the low penalty for guessing wrong, or awareness that weighing many options may not improve the chances of success.

Most managerial decisions therefore emerge as satisficing, mixed with some effort at being a little more rational. Only when the stakes are truly exceptional is there usually some attempt to go beyond straight guessing.

Even using elaborate decision-making methods, you can seldom accurately predict all the consequences from a particular choice. You may have done the calculations, gathered all the available facts, studied and compared all the options yet the outcome still proves different to expectations. How else can one explain all those expensive failed mergers and acquisitions around the world?

All this suggests that you will be better with a rather different decision-making approach from the ultra-rational one usually thrust at new or inexperienced managers.

Essential decision-making behaviour

In a 1999 charity auction for life-sized, black and white fibre-glass cows intense rivalry surfaced for the artist-designed objects and over-bidding led to crazy prices for the cattle. It was a classic case of dangerous competitive arousal, which also affects managers when they go in single-minded pursuit of victory.

Rivalry, time pressures and being in the limelight may all reinforce each other to distort decision making. In fact, the brighter the spotlight, the greater the potential for competitive arousal and bad decisions. Be alert to the potentially harmful dynamics of competitive arousal and make sure your decision making occurs in a more ordered way. Set out to defuse rivalry, reduce the time pressures and deflect the spotlight.

Intuition, as we have seen already, plays a vital role in most decision making. While intuition can seem magical, it mainly relies on using knowledge based on experience. When being intuitive you move knowledge from your unconscious to your conscious mind, which is why sleeping on it before finally deciding makes sense.

You do not learn intuitive decision making so much as tap into this human capacity with four steps:

1 Preparation – get some knowledge or experience.

2 Incubation – allow your mind time to ruminate over the choices.

3 Illumination – arrive at a realisation.

4 Verification – check the realisation using your rational mind.

Based on the above and the evidence from how managers actually make sound decisions the best approach is to:

◆ get fully involved in your decisions

◆ tap into and trust your emotions

◆ use your natural ability to reason.

Ego

When your job so clearly depends on making a good decision, why would anyone knowingly make a bad one? The choice has nothing to do with numbers or even lack of information. What often gets in the way is a misguided determination to make a mark by doing something dramatic. Many managers want to be remembered for having changed the company in a significant way.

When it comes to decision making, therefore, keep a close check on your ego – make choices because they are right for the organisation, not because they will impress others.

Involvement

Teams and groups often make collective decisions they would not have taken individually. This phenomenon, called group think, is both common and potentially dangerous. One well-known CEO regularly adjourned meetings where everyone seemed to be supporting a particular decision. He valued a diversity of opinion and insisted on another meeting 'to get some constructive disagreement going'.

Keep a watch for signs of group think, where everyone seems to agree, with concerted heads nodding, rather than a diversity of views. In the global consultancy Accenture, for example, an anti group think technique used in certain group discussions only allows people who disagree to speak, not those who agree.

On tap or on top?

Could the route to better decision making be to call in the experts to reinforce your opinions or make sense of complicated choices? It might just work, but this puts them on top, rather than on tap, and extensive research into the ability of experts to make predictions shows they suffer from an important deficiency: they fail to learn from experience. Curiously, only two expert groups seemed actively to learn from experience – weather forecasters and bridge players, mainly because they get instant feedback.

only two expert groups seemed actively to learn from experience

Since you will probably make only a few really important big decisions in your entire management career it could be years before you discover whether you made the right one. So learning from your mistakes may be of only limited use.

Without simply passing the entire decision-making task to an expert, a sound approach is to require a risk assessment. Here the use of experts may prove effective for exploring questions such as:

◆ How *big* is the risk we run with this choice?

◆ What is the likelihood or *probability* of a particular outcome occurring?

◆ How could we *reduce* or even eliminate the risk?

◆ What is the *worst-case* scenario?

Formal decision-making systems use risk in a particular way. Rather than concluding an outcome is uncertain, risk assessment tries to quantify the extent of this uncertainty – the chances of something happening. But while there may be all kinds of sophisticated probability calculations, ultimately the final assessment still comes down to an informed guess.

Proper risk analysis is therefore a numerate discipline involving applied mathematics and numerous statistical techniques. Few busy managers have time to become experts in it, which is why calling in an expert may sometimes prove to be justified.

Scenarios

Scenarios help make sense of tricky choices by systematically exploring what might happen if everything goes badly wrong. Using them often drains the decision situation of its mystery and ability to generate excessive fear.

What happens if we launch this product as planned?

◆ Worst-case scenario: it fails dramatically, costing large amounts of money and prestige.

◆ Best-case scenario: it succeeds beyond our wildest dreams.

◆ Most likely scenario: it goes reasonably well, providing a possibility for further investment.

What happens if I confront this person about their persistent lateness?

◆ Worst-case scenario: they become angry, storm out and file a case for constructive dismissal, bullying and discrimination.

◆ Best-case scenario: they acknowledge the problem and completely transform their timekeeping.

◆ Most likely scenario: they reluctantly agree it is an issue and start making noticeable improvements.

What happens if we discount to match the prices offered by our main competitor?

◆ Worst-case scenario: we start a price war which we lose, because we cannot match their resources; key customers defect and we suffer a large drop in profitability.

◆ Best-case scenario: we annihilate the opposition, attracting many of their best customers and put their whole strategy in doubt.

◆ Most likely scenario: no further reductions are made by either side and our market share remains unchanged; profitability gradually returns to normal.

Decision kit bag

Experienced decision makers gradually accumulate their own store of usable methods. Many include the earlier point about trusting gut instinct, while underpinning it with solid data.

Knowing the tools you might adopt in different situations will assist your decision making, enabling you to evolve your own kit bag of possible ways to make important choices.

The following box is not a definitive list and you do not need to master everything. However, discovering how and when to use each method could prove useful in your decision making. Do so either through further reading or by attending a decision-making workshop.

Decision kit bag

The following methods could help you in your decision making but don't get distracted by reams of numbers and analysis if the basic principles, assumptions or conclusions seem to defy common sense.

◆ **Statistical methods** are varied and include averages, dispersion, indices, time series, sampling, regression and probability distributions.

◆ **Decision models** simulate different situations, allowing you to alter the various parameters to see the possible outcomes. Many of the best models rely on using spreadsheets.

◆ **Linear programming** is a statistical technique that takes into account the various constraints affecting important choices.

◆ **Pareto analysis** is used for choosing the most effective changes to make.

◆ **Grid analysis** is used for making a choice involving many factors.

◆ **Decision tree analysis** provides a visual structure in which to lay out options and investigate possible outcomes.

◆ **Force field analysis** identifies forces to strengthen or weaken in attempting to make a particular decision work.

◆ **SWOT analysis** brings together a more holistic picture of the decision options through examining the Strengths, Weaknesses, Opportunities and Threats from different courses of action.

◆ **Cost–benefit appraisals** provide a systematic way of quantifying the likely costs and returns from a particular decision, often where actual numerical data is in short supply.

A fine distinction

Situational analysis offers one of the best approaches to rational decision making. It recognises important differences between a decision, a problem and a plan. Each has slightly different implications for how you approach them, what kind of information you gather and what action you take.

In situational analysis, a problem is something that has already occurred and a deviation from what you wanted or expected to happen. This does not require a decision so much as unravelling what happened and possible remedial action. Problems may eventually have simple solutions, but many involve so much complexity they may not have an easy answer or indeed any at all. By contrast, a plan shows the steps for reaching a particular goal in the future. It requires you to map out the route and anticipate problems along the way.

a plan shows the steps for reaching a particular goal in the future

Finally, a decision involves choices, and the need to generate and evaluate alternatives. Many managers have trained in situational analysis, often called the Kepner–Tregoe method.

Despite the natural tendency to satisfice (see above), there can be no real decision without some choices, even if they are never fully considered. With no viable alternatives, decision making becomes irrelevant. For example, if cleaning food counters must be to national standards of hygiene, there can be little sense debating alternatives.

Making it stick

Most decisions that go wrong do so not from careless analysis, insufficient alternatives, and lack of information or even bad judgement. The most common reasons are insufficient support across the organisation and failure to follow through.

Making consistently sound decisions requires you to be open to alternative views by involving other people in the process. You need to know the truth about your impending decision but people must trust that you will not see them as negative or disloyal. You may need to find ingenious ways to ensure you hear frank opinions.

In the search for making the decision stick, consider asking:

◆ 'Whose help do I need to make it happen?'

◆ 'What do I need to gain their commitment?'

◆ 'Who could undermine or prevent this decision from being implemented?'

To help answer these questions it can be useful to generate a visual representation to show the relationships between the different stakeholders or influencers.

As you advance

Adapting your decision-making approach as you climb the career ladder may prove particularly challenging. In the early days, you may tend towards directive and command orientated approaches. Yet, as you progress, you will need to adopt a more open style that seeks diversity of opinion and participative decision making.

Research reveals that the most successful managers adapt their decision-making style, while the least successful stagnate because they continue to be directive while trying to be participative, action focused and open to alternatives. The higher you go, the further you get from front-line action and the easier it becomes to lose touch with what is happening in the organisation. Isolated decision making is a killer and explains why many top managers stumble, sometimes fatally.

Evolving how you make decisions so you can engage others in the process will therefore be an important factor in whether you thrive in your management career.

Ways to make decisions

☐ *Get fully involved in your decisions*

☐ *Tap into and trust your emotions*

☐ *Use your natural ability to reason*

☐ *Keep a close check on your ego, make choices that are right for the organisation, not because they will impress others*

☐ *Watch for signs of group think, rather than a diversity of views*

☐ *Consider bringing in an expert on risk assessment if the stakes are high*

☐ *Use scenarios to help make sense of tricky choices*

☐ *Become familiar with the main tools for decision making and what they can do*

☐ *Distinguish between a plan, a decision and a problem and how to approach them*

☐ *Consider who can help make your decisions stick, whose commitment you need and who could undermine them in some way*

☐ *As you progress adapt your decision-making style to be more open and inclusive*

16

Inspire meetings

THE AGENDA LOOKED MUCH THE SAME AS USUAL
with nothing special about date or time. But <u>Location</u>, under-
lined in red, jumped out from the rest of the page: 'We face
a huge challenge this year and our meeting to discuss it starts
beside the Colossus ride at Thorpe Park.'

The average manager attends several dozen meetings a
month and far too many prove to be a waste of time.

◆ **Boredom:** nine out of ten admit to daydreaming during
meetings and at least four confess to actually falling asleep.

◆ **Confusion:** uncertainty about what the meeting will
achieve is common.

◆ **Conflict:** participants seem so busy settling old scores and
winning arguments they never address the job in hand.

◆ **Ego:** one or two people grab the 'airtime', control the
agenda and stop others contributing or getting a hearing.

You can tell an inspiring meeting when everyone feels stimu-
lated to attend and leaves believing it has been worthwhile.
Sometimes an unusual location, like the Colossus ride example,
can bring a meeting alive. In such encounters, people may not

always like what they hear, yet still come away uplifted by the experience and feeling it was worthwhile.

A reputation for running effective, inspiring meetings can enhance your career. Despite the negative image of meetings as mainly unproductive places, you will probably get many things done through them. So it makes sense to become good at the various tasks involved: convening, preparing, chairing, participating and ensuring follow-up.

a reputation for running effective, inspiring meetings can enhance your career

Some managers never master the art of running effective meetings and consequently damage their entire careers. Even if you dislike formal meetings, commit to trying to make them enjoyable and productive. Once people realise you nearly always call worthwhile meetings, with focus, pace and relevance, you will rapidly attract a good attendance.

Why bother?

Zero in on any meeting on your patch that keeps happening regularly and review whether it really is necessary. Ritualised sessions, such as a weekly team gathering, may feel reassuring yet can acquire a life of its own with people going through the motions and never really making anything happen.

Lack of focus is a sure way to create dud meetings. Multiple topics and heavy agendas may look impressive, but people soon feel overwhelmed and unsure of what they can achieve. To tighten up on purpose establish a single headline that sums up what the meeting is about. 'Before starting can we just clarify the purpose of this meeting?' This simple request can transform meetings riddled with vague intentions into something more concrete. Hearing the reply you may find occasionally that you can respond: 'In that case, I don't think I should be here,' and leave.

Once people detect your readiness to withdraw unless there is clarity of purpose, they tend to ensure it exists before inviting you. This is one way you can start affecting how the organisation handles its meetings.

Come prepared

Preparation remains the Achilles' heel of many managers. Never assume your mere presence justifies a meeting. Make time to prepare well: for example, read papers sent for discussion, talk to people in advance about the issues, collect information and begin formulating your views.

Once people realise you normally do your homework they will tend to listen more carefully, giving your views more weight. With good preparation, you will feel more confident to listen openly while being careful to show you have not already made up your mind.

Attendance

Devote time to ensuring the right people attend because their contribution will be essential or you need their commitment or involvement in some way. Also, watch out for meeting creep, where the number attending escalates through fear of offending certain people or from gatecrashers. Explain why you have chosen specific people to attend. 'I need you there because...' can prove a compelling incentive for people to turn up, even though they are extremely busy.

Manage the agenda

Whoever controls the agenda partly controls the meeting. This underrated skill can save countless wasted hours. Create written agendas, in advance or right at the start, allocating time according to urgency, importance and complexity.

Agendas tend to grow as people add items, many of which may be nice to discuss, yet are not essential. This does not mean excluding any time on pleasant or social discussion; just set some boundaries for this activity. For example, create a parking lot for issues you do not want to discuss now.

Clarify whether each agenda item is for

◆ information only

◆ discussion, or

◆ decision.

Be willing to break with tradition, eliminating long-serving items like any other business (AOB). These tempt people to drone on about their pet idea or even hijack the entire meeting. Invite those with new items to add them to the next agenda. Anything genuinely urgent will usually surface at the start as you seek to clarify the purpose of the gathering. Similarly, rather than the ritual of reading out previous minutes, manage by exception, by checking in advance on previously agreed actions, allowing only those without known follow-through to surface.

seek to clarify the purpose of the gathering

Repeatedly carrying forward items not dealt with causes future agendas to spin out of control. Suggest items returned more than twice be dealt with in one of these ways:

◆ discussed immediately

◆ sent for attention elsewhere, or

◆ dropped entirely.

> ## Good agenda habits
>
> ◆ Aim for a written agenda
>
> ◆ Distribute the agenda in advance
>
> ◆ Explain location, date, start and end times
>
> ◆ Make agenda creation a participative experience
>
> ◆ Agenda items should reach the chairperson well in advance of the meeting
>
> ◆ Start with easy items, put harder items in the middle, and end on an up note
>
> ◆ After each agenda item, summarise the main point, and state what the result/action will be, when it is to be completed, and by whom

Chairing

You do not need to lead every meeting you convene. Often it makes sense to let others do it, while you watch what goes on and play a supporting role. If others lead the session, ensure they acquire the necessary skills. Give them some help with what people expect from a good chairperson.

If you do chair the meeting, take responsibility for ensuring that everyone receives airtime, and make it clear you expect to hear from everyone.

Note taking and minutes

Whoever takes on this role needs to understand about action minutes. These simply record what the meeting agreed should happen next. Strongly resist discursive commentary about who said what at the meeting as this leads to lengthy minutes attempting to capture everything that occurred. When, however, multiple teams work on a project, it may be useful occasionally to show the reason for a decision or the context for some action.

Time keeping

Meetings that start and end promptly rapidly acquire a sound reputation. Keep reviewing the pace of the meeting so if the discussion drifts you can take action quickly. Invite everyone to help the meeting stay focused. You might even agree a group visual signal that people can use to suggest the discussion is heading off course.

Five minutes before the end, warn attendees of the amount of time left: it will help people refocus. Consider appointing someone to keep track of the time and to give feedback regularly on this aspect.

Late arrivals

These interrupt meetings and undermine good time keeping. Be willing to explain that you expect people to be punctual as a sign of respect for everyone's time.

Avoid confronting latecomers in public and never assume their behaviour stems from laziness or a desire to be awkward. Perhaps they have important care duties at home before leaving, face a particularly difficult commute or have some other solid reason. Privately enquire about the reasons as simply asking the question may result in them arriving on time in future. If someone keeps arriving late for no good reason, give them the role of meeting timekeeper. After doing this for a while they will naturally tend to arrive on time.

Are you inadvertently encouraging late arrivals? For instance, by always starting your meetings late to accommodate them, you punish the rest who arrived promptly. Similarly, by offering late arrivals a full summary of the discussion so far you punish the rest who must sit through it, and this rewards anti-social behaviour. If normally late arrivals come on time, publicly thank them; maybe even send a written note appreciating their effort. Give them a role too, such as ensuring the meeting stays on course. This shows you have renewed confidence in them. When late arrivals try to slip into the meeting unnoticed, stop the meeting and welcome them, but also tactfully invite them to apologise to everyone else if they do not offer one without prompting.

Two last-resort measures:

1 Ask a persistent late arrival not to attend, since this may be what they want in the first place, and be ready to do without them.

2 Publicise and effect a closed-door policy in which no one may enter once the meeting starts. Excluded in this way, people almost always arrive promptly next time.

Finally, get tough about timing and most people will welcome it.

Control the environment

Many meetings happen informally in a coffee area or casually in the corridor in which case you cannot do much about the environment. But for formal meetings make sure the environment contributes to an effective experience. For instance, are there avoidable distractions such as stunning views outside, poor lighting, uncomfortable seating or refreshments due to arrive at the wrong time?

Contributions

Calling a meeting where most people sit entirely silent most of the time makes little sense. Inspiring meetings involve everyone, even if they cannot all speak for long.

inspiring meetings involve everyone

Large meetings can be daunting and deter some people from contributing, even if they feel strongly about an issue. Equally, small meetings can inhibit contributions because people feel every word they utter will come under scrutiny. Try breaking participants into smaller groups to discuss an issue for a few minutes, and then invite a response from each person. Alternatively, ask the group to summarise its views, rather than putting the onus on any one person to comment.

If you invite people to arrive with a considered response to an issue, you will also encourage their contribution. You then go round systematically seeking everyone's input. When people contribute, give them your total attention. People soon notice if the manager seems bored or distracted, so stay fully alert.

You can also promote more participation by inviting people to express their objections in a positive, rather than a negative way. Coach everyone to watch out for that destructive phrase: 'Yes but...'.

Handle conflict

It can be scary chairing a meeting – people expect you to handle tension, confrontation and disagreements. Not everyone feels comfortable with this, yet it is all part of becoming a successful manager. How do you tend to react to public conflict? Does it worry you? Is it something you try to avoid or prefer to smooth over? Or do you become forceful, even aggressive. (See also Chapter 3.)

The secret of handling conflict in meetings is straightforward. First of all, allow it to surface. Having spotted a potential conflict, act positively and ask attendees if they want to deal with the issue on the spot. If so, insist on a full airing of the pros and cons.

Handling conflict, though, also means being willing to deal with feelings. Try asking yourself:

◆ What does the speaker mean, not just the spoken words?

◆ What is the speaker feeling?

◆ What are the other people in the meeting feeling?

These questions can help you diagnose what is happening and to decide what to do next.

Inspire

People look to their manager to hold inspiring meetings, not dull gatherings where routine triumphs over involvement.

You may need to develop ways to lift a meeting, energising people and tapping into their natural creativity so they want to take part. Encouraging full participation can be one way to inspire and another is to keep trying new ways to win people's interest and attention.

New ways to try

◆ Rather than sticking to the same format each time, try experimenting with an entirely new one. For example, you could limit the meeting to one item only and ask everyone to prepare in depth.

◆ Try a fast-and-furious agenda one day, with no item allowed more than say five minutes airtime, or invite people to raise their issues by drawing a picture of them with coloured pens or even paints.

◆ Consider holding the entire meeting with everyone standing. One likely consequence is that it will prove admirably short!

◆ Convene the meeting entirely off-site or at an usual place such as a park, a customer's office, an art gallery or a room not normally used for meetings.

Quite simply, use your imagination, and invite the attendees to suggest ways to enliven and make their meeting more rewarding.

Ways to run inspiring meetings

☐ *Invest your personal time in good preparation for your meetings*

☐ *For each meeting ensure there is clarity and good practice about:*

  – *purpose*

  – *attendance*

  – *the agenda*

  – *chairing*

  – *note taking and minutes*

  – *timekeeping*

  – *late arrivals*

  – *the environment*

☐ *Make sure everyone can become involved, receiving enough airtime*

☐ *Encourage participation by breaking participants into smaller groups*

☐ *Stay fully involved, giving people your full attention*

☐ *Coach people to avoid the destructive 'Yes but...' syndrome*

☐ *Get comfortable dealing with conflict; allow it to surface and, where appropriate, tackle it head on*

☐ *Experiment with ways to lift a meeting, energising people and tapping into their natural creativity so they want to participate*

☐ *Keep meetings fresh with new formats, new places to meet and other creative ideas*

17

Encourage creativity and innovation

ERIC SCHMIDT DREAMS OF ORGANISING the entire world's information. Google's Executive Chairman estimates it will take his company 300 years to achieve it. With that perspective, Google managers can afford to be extraordinarily patient. They know it will involve constant betting on ideas, without worrying much about the likely return on investment.

Managing for creativity and innovation sits right at the top of Google's organisational agenda. Many other companies also realise that in the longer term, this is the best way to ensure success. Short term they can tweak what they have already. 'Innovation is our lifeblood: we expect everyone to do it', says Procter & Gamble, which embeds it in the whole organisation and does not rely solely on traditional research and development.

Even if you do not feel particularly creative and have never innovated anything, it is still a core part of your management role to harvest suggestions, generate ideas and encourage fresh thinking, particularly within your own team.

But why do so many smart, hardworking managers in well-run companies find it impossible to innovate successfully?

Researchers have long puzzled over this situation and blame several culprits such as:

◆ excessive attention on the company's most profitable customers

◆ creating new products and services that do little to help customers

◆ financial tools such as discounted cash and net present value, that underestimate the real returns and benefits of proceeding with investments in innovation.

Often, though, it comes down to some simple factors that you can tackle wherever you are in the organisation. For example, people often expect innovation to mean some sensational breakthrough that will change everything in its wake. In practice most innovation occurs through a steady application of small improvements, one piled on the other until the cumulative effect of this creativity makes its impact.

Hard work, not genius

To encourage creativity and innovation you may need to abandon some conventional ideas about being a manager. For example, it could mean rewarding failure, not having strict targets and accepting loss of control over how people spend their time. IBM summed it up years ago: 'If you want to double your successes, double your failures.'

you may need to abandon some conventional ideas about being a manager

Creative geniuses usually reject the notion that what they do requires an innate talent, or depends on having the right genes. Twyla Tharp, one of the world's great choreographers and author of a book on creativity, for example, talks of it as a pragmatic, almost businesslike endeavour. She argues it relies on systematic hard work, rather than sudden, blinding inspiration.

To encourage creativity amongst your colleagues you will
need to:

◆ capture good ideas

◆ keep ideas alive

◆ find new uses for old ideas

◆ put promising ideas to the test

◆ eliminate blocks that may deter breakthroughs.

All seemingly sensible but, in practice, how do you go about
doing them? Here are some of the ways you can be proactive.

Hiring

IDEO, the company that helps clients innovate through
design, once interviewed someone with lots of great ideas
about computers and the arts. No one knew how to use him,
but they hired him all the same. Eventually, he generated an
unexpected and highly profitable area of development.

In Maynard Leigh Associates, we have often encountered
candidates with strange skills and interests outside our own
experience or even immediate needs. Who would have thought,
for example, that the man who loved skulls and ferrets would
become one of our most valued employees, able to solve most
practical problems, from faulty air conditioners to uncovering
strange software for our idiosyncratic requirements.

Imaginative hiring decisions can be a way to promote creativity and innovation in your patch and beyond.

Live with failure

'Please fail very quickly – so you can try again,' is how Google's
one-time CEO puts it, underpinning this with ensuring a high
tolerance of risk.

Instructed to abandon an apparently unsuccessful display monitor he was developing, an engineer in Hewlett-Packard went ahead and showed it to customers, eventually producing a massively successful product line. Some years later, HP publicly and apologetically awarded him a medal for 'extraordinary contempt and defiance beyond the normal call of engineering duty'.

Living with failure seems the exact opposite of what management is about – bringing order out of chaos. Yet companies with an enviable innovation record allow many flowers to bloom and accept failure as the inevitable price of success.

You probably feel comfortable offering praise and rewarding people for success and penalising inaction. Yet you may also need to get used to rewarding people for failing. Failure is how individuals and companies learn.

failure is how individuals and companies learn

The other side of the coin of living with failure is the constant drive to experiment. What sets Toyota's culture apart is the way it encourages employees to be forthcoming about the mistakes they make. By encouraging open communications as a core value, Toyota has made its culture remarkably tolerant of failure.

Build innovation into job descriptions

In companies like 3M, P&G, Google, and some Japanese companies, everyone's job description contains a requirement to innovate or be creative. However expressed, whether as constantly seeking improvements or always seeking new ideas, the core message is that everyone needs to be inventive at work. Expecting innovation from everyone, though, works best with satisfied, motivated employees who realise their own managers and supervisors will take their suggestions seriously.

Encourage shootouts

In ITV plc, a 14-person internal unit called ITV Imagine has the remit to incubate ideas or concepts from staff and to gather external knowledge and expertise on national and global trends and technology. As its founder Bruce Robertson puts it: 'We needed to find a way to protect ideas and stop them from being killed off or categorised and narrowed.'

One of the most vital ingredients to look for in assessing and pursuing new ideas is who has the energy to pursue them. If you cannot decide which new projects or new ideas to bet on based on objective data, at least select on the basis of ones that have the most committed supporters.

You can promote creativity and innovation by encouraging situations where ideas must fight it out in public. This is not the same as encouraging personality clashes or relationship conflicts. Instead, you make people present their ideas for public scrutiny and get people arguing about them.

Challenge the structure

Toyota's competitors famously excused its success on, first, an undervalued yen, then a docile workforce, followed by Japanese culture, and finally superior automation. Eventually, though, came the realisation that Toyota had learned how to gain more from its front-line workers than other companies. It used a disciplined process for turning them into problem solvers, innovators and change agents.

Gary Hamel, author of a farsighted book on the future of management, takes an informed and highly-critical view of conventional management. He argues that the best managers in the future will be those who know how to innovate, finding entirely new ways to lead, coordinate and motivate.

Management innovation allows companies to reach new levels of performance and differs from basic product or service innovation. It challenges convention but requires discipline to succeed. For example, how much freedom do your people actually possess to try new ways of doing things? Are they so constrained by rules and conventions that there is little chance of anything more effective and productive emerging? How could you bend the rules, alter the constraints, release the energy to invent? What might be getting in the way of them becoming innovators? If you do not know, try asking them. Invite them to explore with you what it would take to release their potential to come up with new ways of working, thinking and doing.

Look for the obstacles that your organisation erects to stop or slow fresh thinking, experimentation and the willingness to fail. Having identified them be active in trying to minimise or eliminate their effects. A 2008 global study by the Hays Group found most executives (80 per cent) say innovation is a top three priority but only one in five say they feel able to do it.

You could also face an uphill struggle to encourage creativity and innovation if your organisation unwittingly creates blocks to breakthroughs. In most companies, innovation remains the exclusive job of certain individuals, while only about 6 per cent are innovation democracies in which everyone gets a chance to be creative and make breakthroughs.

Spotting

From penicillin to Post-it Notes so many breakthroughs arise from people seeing possibilities, rather than the actual innovation itself. Spotting new ideas and realising their

hone your spotting skills

potential can be as important as devising the ideas in the first place. Great spotters always outperform actual creators.

No matter how creative you can be personally, the world will always produce far more ideas than any single individual will. So hone your spotting skills!

The first step in honing is staying deeply connected with the core purpose. What do you want innovation to achieve? What is the need for it? Why does it matter so much?

Many great innovations die because no one makes a connection between the idea and its eventual outlet. To spot great ideas waiting to explode look for the following.

Unexpected happenings

These can be highly productive sources to prompt new ideas because most people dismiss them as accidental, disregard them or resent them.

Use the unexpected as a trigger for creative discussion and ways to relook at 'how we do things round here'.

Incongruities

Gaps between expectations and results can be a rich source of fresh and innovative thinking. The famous invention of the Post-it Note stemmed from the failure of the original glue to work as expected.

Use 'what went wrong?' and 'what can we do about this?' as triggers for new thinking.

Industry and market changes

Structural changes can offer opportunities for innovation almost overnight. The fortunes of many dotcom companies, for example Amazon and the social website evolution, stemmed from this realisation.

Keep reviewing how shifts in the environment offer new ways of behaving and being and have implications for existing products and services.

Demographic shifts

This can generate innovation opportunities, as these changes, while heavily data driven, still need imaginative interpretation.

Realising an ageing population meant it would become harder to recruit young people, companies like B&Q have innovated by hiring older workers, well beyond normal retirement.

Take known demographic trends and extrapolate them a few years into the future to assess their likely impact on the organisation, and what it does and how it does it.

Changes in perception

Changes in mood, beliefs and attitude can offer enormous opportunities to innovate.

As the mobile phone evolved into an everyday object that everyone should own, it provided a large arena for companies to innovate and use their creativity. A trend against disposable plastic bags offered new opportunities for existing companies to both save on packaging and sell longer-life bags.

Look for current alterations in perceptions as a place to explore the opportunities to innovate and change.

Revealing stories

These can be a great source of creativity and innovation.

When you hear of an inspiring story at work, what does it tell you? What lessons does it suggest for the future? How could you use this to generate some new action or direction?

Managing the creatives

Every company has its share of exceptionally creative people, ones who thrive on being different, in challenging the system and in getting their kicks from doing something entirely new. The most difficult ones to manage are the mavericks, those hard to handle, talented people who don't quite fit in and persist in coming up with ideas and views that challenge conventional wisdom. However, as Anita Roddick, the founder of the Body Shop once pointed out: 'Find the mavericks and you will uncover your company's future.'

It is much easier to kill creativity than to support it – not because of a vendetta against it, but because organisations love coordination, productivity and control. These develop their own momentum, which can crush new ideas or experiments. Some managers also fear creativity and what it may unleash, and with some justification. Mobilising huge amounts of innovative thinking and constant creative chatter seldom delivers practical organisational results.

For all its much vaunted creative flair, Apple actually avoids too much creativity. The hierarchy around the top performers looks flat, but when they make decisions they expect them to be implemented with little questioning. As one commentator puts it: 'They have no interest in watching 1000 flowers of innovation bloom all over the company. Employees are not empowered to make a difference. They are expected to do a clearly defined job and do it as well as they can.'

The lesson from Apple is not perhaps to confine creativity and innovation to a select few, but to ensure there is also a steady focus on implementation. To spark innovation you may need to re-think how you and your colleagues respond to it, motivate, reward and assign work to people.

Managing the bright sparks

◆ Acknowledge their knowledge – make them feel special while making sure they stay connected.

◆ Win resources and give them space – clever people want and need these to succeed.

◆ Be an umbrella – help the bright sparks cope with the organisational bureaucracy, shielding them from its worst excesses.

◆ Congratulate failure – clever people live on the edge of failure, not all innovations work.

◆ Give direction – make sure your bright sparks do not disappear up their own goals; help them stay related to those of the organisation.

◆ Listen to the silences – getting the best from them requires you to develop your situation-sensing skills; that is, the ability to assess morale, commitment and individual motivation.

◆ Be accessible – listen hard to the needs of your bright sparks. Your message should be: 'I am available and you are important.'

◆ Encourage outside recognition – they cannot live by internal appreciation alone. They are encouraged by recognition from outside, for example by awards for the best research paper and so on.

◆ Simplify the environment for them – all organisations have rules but bright sparks thrive under an absence of rules and the rules need to be agreed, for example those involving risks.

◆ Don't expect gratitude – clever people often resist leadership, so do not expect thanks for getting it right.

◆ Discover people's inner passion – both to solve problems and do things they believe are new and worthwhile.

Finally, beware of compulsive idea generation. Mobilising huge amounts of innovative thinking and constant creative chatter seldom delivers practical organisational results. For purposeful action, make sure there is a steady focus on implementation. In short, stop people just talking about it and start doing it.

Ways to manage innovation and creativity

☐ *Use imaginative hiring decisions*

☐ *Reward those who insist on doing things their own way and like being different*

☐ *Allow your people space and time to explore ways of being creative and innovative*

☐ *Provide situations where new ideas must fight it out in public*

☐ *In making sense of new ideas examine who has the energy to pursue them*

☐ *Search out and destroy, or try to minimise, the blocks to creativity and new ideas*

☐ *To promote new thinking start with a problem that has large consequences, and one that stirs the soul*

☐ *Search for opportunities that offer potential breakthroughs, such as unexpected happenings, incongruities, industry and market changes, demographic shifts, and changes in perception*

☐ *Review how you motivate, reward and assign work to people – do these encourage or deter fresh thinking?*

☐ *Manage your creative talent to maximise its effectiveness*

☐ *Deter excessive talk about creativity and help people focus on doing it*

18

Select and recruit

'WE LIKE MR FRIENDLY, Mr Ambitious and Mr Faithful, but we don't like Mr Grumpy, Mr Lazy or Mr Dishonest,' explains MD John Timpson at an HRD conference. He was talking about his firm's approach to recruitment (reported in *People Management*, May 2008). The company tells its interviewers to associate a candidate's personality with a character similiar to that from the Mr Men children's series. Timpson's unusual approach probably works a lot better than many of the conventional recruitment techniques companies employ. The company knows who it needs to recruit and wants everyone to be sure about how to do it.

If you happen to be a manager in one of the most successful companies in the world, which of course you may well be, recruitment and selection will almost certainly mean 'getting the right people on the bus'. This is far more proactive than simply filling the occasional vacancy and emerged from a seminal study into how truly outstanding organisations and their managers approach selection and recruitment (see *Good to Great* by Jim Collins). What all these companies had in common was their unwavering commitment to finding and hiring the right people, and *only then* deciding on exactly where they wanted the bus to go: that is, what they most wanted the company to achieve.

Doing it well

To get the right people on the bus though, many organisations often continue an unhappy tradition of poor recruitment practices. As Henry Stewart, founder of Happy, a leading IT training company and winner of several best employer awards complains: 'One of the things that really gets me mad is that most recruiting is absolutely terrible' (*People Management*, 20 March 2008).

What exactly goes wrong? Basic errors include:

◆ not knowing who you need to recruit

◆ not knowing why you need to recruit them

◆ overreliance on interviews for selection

◆ excessive trust of reference checks, or making none at all

◆ use of highly dubious personality tests

◆ poor interviewing skills.

Consequently, many appointments fail to live up to expectations. That is putting it mildly. In fact, an estimated half of all senior-level appointments end in a firing or resignation and at lower levels the record may be even worse. One reason for such bad outcomes is excluding the right talent in the first place.

Wasting half your available talent seems so obviously wrong, yet entire countries, let alone companies, still do it. Unwilling to see half the nation's potential wasted any longer, in early 2006 the Norwegian government made a dramatic decision. To avoid the risk of dissolution, it became mandatory for public companies to change the composition of their boards in favour of more women. The country subsequently set a global record for the highest proportion of female non-executive directors (*The Guardian*, 6 March 2008). Around the developed world managers complain they cannot find the right talent, while ignoring the potential already available to them both within and beyond the organisation.

Outside recruitment agencies now often handle the administrative chore of creating a shortlist. While apparently a cost-effective approach, it may also cut you off from spotting talent that does not fit neatly into the job description to hand. Because of their passion to 'get the right people on the bus' the best managers take a close interest in the recruitment process.

> *the best managers take a close interest in the recruitment process*

The process

Faced with a vacancy in your team you may naturally be anxious to fill it. Yet this may miss the bigger picture, since sensible recruiting starts with the organisation's, or a division's, business plan. From this flows the rest of the process.

Recruitment process

1 Create a business plan – identify company or divisional aims.

2 Analyse the need – identify numbers and types of people, skills and other human resource requirements.

3 Analyse jobs – specify the new work and decide content; prepare job descriptions.

4 Draw up candidate specifications – describe the sort of person who would fit the job.

5 Attract candidates – publicise vacancies.

▶

6   Sort applicants – make initial shortlists matching candidates to requirements, shortlisting who to take to the next stage.

7   Select for interview – meet candidates, test and interview.

8   Decide and appoint – formally by letter.

9   Induce the chosen candidate – the first few months are critical for making people feel connected and setting expectations.

Why recruit?

By holding the bigger picture, you position yourself as able to think and act beyond your immediate role. It means pursuing answers to questions such as:

◆ What does the organisation want to be?

◆ What are its aspirations?

◆ What is its strategic intent?

◆ What future capabilities will the organisation need?

These help focus on the strategic aspect of recruiting. International research consistently shows a large proportion of people at work feel underused, disengaged or alienated. The figure can be as high as 8 out of 10 employees who feel underused. The results suggest the value of a strategic approach where you first look hard for the resources you need from within, even when it means developing them to the level required.

There is also research evidence that star performers brought in from outside seldom live up to expectations. So, apart from the above strategic questions, your initial recruitment question needs to be: 'Do we have someone internal who can do this work?' While offering fresh energy, expertise and perspective, outsiders take longer to adjust to the prevailing culture than those recruited internally. If you are trying to change culture though, external people may fit in more easily.

Who do we need?

Failure to get the right person on the bus often stems from confusion about the sort of person needed, which is why the slightly bizarre Timpson approach mentioned earlier makes sense. At least the company seems clear about people it does *not* want to employ.

Lengthy job descriptions with their lists of tasks seldom prove decisive during actual recruitment. Instead, aim for a broad, yet accurate, picture of the *intent* behind the job. What do you want this person to do? What are the essential areas of responsibility? For example:

◆ manage the help desk and ensure it deals promptly and well with all requests

◆ handle all press enquiries and build good relations with the media.

Short, clear work descriptions, rather than pages of tasks, will best support your recruitment process.

Check also whether the prevailing recruitment system treats everyone who applies with equality and respect. For example, does everyone contacting the company in search of a job always receive a friendly reply? Are job adverts worded so they attract all available talent?

Finally, even when issuing a general rejection check on its approach. Does it show respect and perhaps wish the person good luck in their search for another job, rather than a few clinical lines of dismissal?

even when issuing a general rejection check on its approach

The interview trap

Most managers believe they are good at interviewing even though research evidence suggests otherwise. One reason is that unstructured interviews prove to be poor predictors of success when used as the main means of hiring. Rather than relying mainly on interviews, some organisations take prospective employees through a condensed, two-hour training module to see if the candidate can support others and has the potential to learn and train colleagues.

You can increase your chances of selection success by using the following long-standing guidelines.

◆ Structure interviews into a logical sequence covering key areas.

◆ Rather than relying on attitude questions, such as 'How do you feel about... ?', instead ask behaviour and situation questions, such as 'What would you do if...?' and 'How would you deal with...?'

◆ Identify those critical questions that can rapidly exclude or include someone: for example, 'If you were offered the job would you take it?'

◆ Avoid relying solely on the interview as your main means of selection.

Interviewing seems easy because apparently you merely fire questions at your victim. In practice, most people need to develop their interviewing skills to gain confidence, reduce bias and avoid the halo effect (see below, page 241).

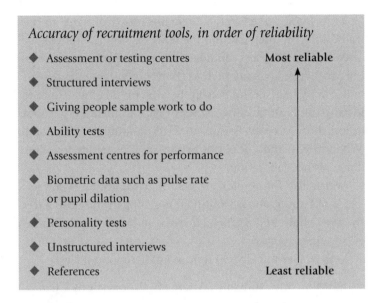

Accuracy of recruitment tools, in order of reliability

- Assessment or testing centres   **Most reliable**
- Structured interviews
- Giving people sample work to do
- Ability tests
- Assessment centres for performance
- Biometric data such as pulse rate or pupil dilation
- Personality tests
- Unstructured interviews
- References   **Least reliable**

Spot the liar

The 2008 winner of *The Apprentice* reality show publicly admitted lying in his CV. Unfortunately for the cause of integrity, being untruthful in this case did not prove fatal to his selection.

Imagine you have three fresh CVs in front of you. How many will contain lies and inaccuracies? According to a 2003 study by the Risk Advisory Group, of CVs submitted by job applicants, two out of three cannot be fully trusted. To spot dodgy CVs look for gaps in the person's life story, then dig into the accuracy of claims made about skills, knowledge or qualifications.

Even without the CV, there remains plenty of scope to mislead during an interview. But the body cannot lie, and you will often be able to detect candidate cover-ups. For example, listen for negative statements such as 'I am not an anxious person', rather than 'I am a calm person'. Be alert for missing details, for instance not volunteering names or gaps in their story. Follow up on short answers. For instance, responding 'Quite a lot' to 'What do you know about our company?' may hide ignorance if there is no elaboration.

Watch also for physical clues such as squirming in the seat, a lack of hand gestures, continual touching of the nose, excessive eye contact and a general increase in the number of speech errors and nervous tics.

Verbal clues to help you to root out deception include:

◆ how long the candidate takes to answer questions – liars generally go on for longer

◆ slow and very considered speech – the candidate is thinking ahead, perhaps to avoid self-revelations (though watch out for someone suffering from a speech defect)

◆ fast, high-pitched speech as way of glossing over something

◆ anxious to fill in pauses between questions, as if having something to hide.

Generally, the less prepared someone is for an interview the more they will reveal the tell-tale signs.

Generic questions

you can ask anything so long as it is central

Anti-discrimination legislation and the requirement to ensure fairness means you need to become fully aware of what you can and cannot reasonably ask in an interview. As a general guideline, you can ask anything so long as it is central to the person doing the job effectively.

To develop your structured interview, create a focus on some or all of the following issues.

◆ Ability in current or past positions – does the person have the technical skills to handle the role?
'Describe your working day.'
'What are your three most important responsibilities in your present or last position?'
'Tell me about a problem you found difficult to handle and why.'

◆ Ability to adapt – how flexible is this person?
'Can you give examples of where you have changed in response to situations at work?'
'Describe a time when your boss asked you to do something that initially seemed beyond you, and what you did.'

◆ Motivation – what drives the candidate?
'What personal qualities will you need to make a success in the job you are applying for?'
'What have you done in your current job that you are most proud of?'

◆ Communication skills – does the person have the necessary interpersonal skills, especially for roles interacting with customers, whether internal or external?
'Tell me about a time when you went out of your way to satisfy a customer, a client or a colleague at work.'
'What departments do you have day-to-day dealings with?'
'What difficulties have you encountered, and how did you handle them?'

◆ Decision-making skills – does the person show they can make sensible work choices, no matter how limited their role?
'Tell me about an unpopular choice you have made at work.'
'What kinds of decisions are hardest for you?'
'Describe a situation where you needed to think on your feet or adapt quickly.'

◆ Organisational skills – the ability of the candidate to organise their workload productively.
  'Tell me about a goal you set recently; what have you done to reach it?'
  'Describe a time when you failed to reach a goal; what did you learn from that?'
  'What do you do to relieve stress at work?'
  'How do you go about planning your day?'

◆ Coolness under fire – can this person handle stress and show composure when under pressure?
  'What is the most difficult situation you have faced?'
  'How did you react?'
  'Tell me about a situation where there were objections to your ideas.'
  'Tell me about an occasion when your performance did not live up to your managers' expectations – how did you handle the criticism?'

◆ Manageability – is this person likely to respond well to being managed?
  'When your manager gives you directions what is your general reaction?'
  'What are some of the things about which you and your manager disagree?'
  'In what areas could your manager have done a better job in managing you?'

◆ Candidate preferences – what kind of management style does this person respond to best?
  'How did your manager get the best from you?'
  'Describe your manager's strengths.'
  'Tell me about the best manager you have had; what made this person exceptional?'

◆ Loyalty – does the candidate have a sense of duty to their
  employer, not just servile loyalty?
  'Tell me about a time when you felt it necessary to convince your
  team to do something, such as change a policy or procedure.'
  'How did you go about this?'
  'Has there ever been a time when you went along with a policy
  you did not agree with? Why?'

◆ Self-assessment – what is the candidate's self-perception
  and how did they arrive at this judgement?
  'How would you describe yourself?'
  'What motivates you and why?'
  'What are your plans for future study?'
  'Give me some examples of mistakes you have made in your job;
  what have you learned from them?'

◆ Interest in the job – how keen is this person to come and
  work for you?
  'What attracts you to this position?'
  'What interests you most about us?'
  'Why did you apply for this role?'
  'What do you know about our company?'

Halo and goodbye

A candidate walks in wearing stylish clothes and talks in an
accent suggesting an expensive private education. Depending on
your own background, the immediate impression you gain may
colour every other conclusion you draw about this person, and
perhaps quite wrongly. This is an example of the halo effect at
work, in which unconscious errors or bias can influence your
entire view of a candidate during selection.

The halo effect shapes perception because *the halo effect*
we make inferences about purely subjective *shapes perception*
qualities. We assume a well-dressed person

must be competent or that 'nicely spoken' means they are nice to people they deal with. Both of these may be entirely untrue. So, to counter the halo effect, concentrate on objective factors that can help screen out subjective influences.

Fairness

Even if your organisation has a sophisticated HR support system, take responsibility for ensuring that the recruitment process you become involved with is fair. In particular, be alert to issues of diversity and the need to avoid discrimination of various kinds involving race, sexual orientation, age, gender and disability.

Discrimination and diversity can be tricky and complex areas and there are numerous guides available on these issues. Before attempting to get the right people on the bus, make sure you understand the constraints.

Ways to select and recruit

☐ *Take a close interest in the recruitment process*

☐ *Use strategic questions as part of your recruitment role*

☐ *Review whether and how the business plan relates to the decision to recruit*

☐ *Before recruiting, check whether someone internal could do the work*

☐ *Assess whether you could eliminate, or redistribute the work*

☐ *Develop your interviewing skills in a safe learning environment*

☐ *Avoid relying solely on the interview as your main means of selection*

☐ *Structure interviews into a logical sequence covering key areas*

☐ *In interviews, use behaviour and situation questions, not just attitude questions*

☐ *Identify critical questions that can rapidly exclude or include someone*

☐ *Develop skills to spot clues to root out candidate deception*

☐ *Learn to spot the halo effect, which distorts perceptions of candidates*

☐ *Be aware of discriminatory recruitment practices and how to ensure equal opportunities and encourage diversity*

19

Show integrity

WHAT KEEPS THE BOSS AWAKE AT NIGHT? Forget product failure, fraud or terrorist attack. The big nightmare is reputational risk. One rogue employee's actions can turn an entire enterprise toxic. The most robust organisation may be vulnerable. Arthur Andersen, a global service with revenues of billions, closed within weeks. Collusion in fraud at Enron destroyed an unrivalled standing. Reputational problems escalate at terrifying speed, as executives at News International know only too well.

Systems, procedures, rules of engagement and publicised values do not guarantee protection. The words 'respect, integrity, communication and excellence', for instance, hung in the entrance to Enron. Far more depends on managers who guard the organisation's ethics with fierce pride and ensure others act in similar ways.

Most executives mean to run ethical organisations. Few will deny the importance of integrity and compliance programmes. For example, Partners HealthCare is a not-for-profit, integrated healthcare system in Boston, Massachusetts. Its declared values appear in the box below.

'Partners Health Care is committed to conducting its affairs in accordance with the highest ethical and legal standards. In order to maintain these standards, all those associated with Partners will perform their duties with integrity and honesty.'

Source: *A Guide to Ethical Standards at Partners Health Care.*

To bring such values to life is vital to the business achieving its mission. Yet, elsewhere corruption and dubious business practices remain rife. Organisations train employees to comply with the latest regulatory mandates. So why do these problems persist? In some cases, crooks capture senior roles. Or, individuals subvert rules because their bosses fail to recognise unethical behaviour or do not follow through on ethical issues.

A failure of corporate governance explains why rules are sometimes bent or broken. Ethical issues get downplayed or ignored. The Ford Pinto's defective gas tank is a classic case of managerial responsibility going off the rails. This unsafe part could cause death or injury in a small number of cases. Analysis showed settling law suits was cheaper than spending a few dollars on fixing the fault. So Ford took no remedial action. The executives responsible relied on a 'rational' business analysis, guided by the cost/benefit data. Later, Ford paid millions in damages, suffered expensive product recalls and tarnished its reputation.

often dubious behaviour requires someone in a senior role to raise the alarm

Often dubious behaviour requires someone in a senior role to raise the alarm. To assume that the HR department will do this is a cop-out. Regardless of seniority, every manager is responsible for promoting ethics and doing the right thing. Successful managers need to both understand and know how to support it. You foster decent behaviour when you:

◆ Walk the talk

◆ Show core values drive management decisions

◆ Treat others with respect

◆ Avoid deception, artificiality or shallowness

◆ Know where you stand on issues

◆ Speak up if you observe things going wrong.

Is integrity too vague to matter? (For a review of the various meanings of integrity see *Stanford Encyclopaedia of Philosophy*, 2008, **http://plato.stanford.edu/entries/integrity**). Cursed with a definition problem that has worried philosophers for centuries, managers may wonder whether they should go beyond agreeing: 'it's essential to do the right thing' Could integrity be a 'nice to have' not a 'must have'? To question its relevance, though, is like arguing education is expensive. Try the cost of not having it.

For all its imprecision, integrity is like a precious diamond. It is immutable, hard to alter and part of oneself and the organisation. It has many facets and a one-dimensional interpretation will seldom suffice.

Source: © Maynard Leigh Associates, reproduced by permission.

> ## What is integrity?
>
> From the Latin, meaning *whole* or *complete*:
>
> ◆ Discern right from wrong
>
> ◆ Act on your observations, even at personal cost
>
> ◆ Say you are acting on your understanding of right or wrong

The ripples from major corporate ethics scandals spread far beyond their original starting point. The issue worries even the best-run organisations. A KPMG survey in the US found the frequency of misconduct 'remains high'. In fact, almost three out of four employees spotted serious wrongdoing inside their organisation. Around half (46 per cent) said this meant 'a significant loss of public trust' if revealed.

> *'The bigger the organisation gets the less easy it becomes to keep it honest.'*
>
> (*Future Files: The 5 trends That Will Shape the next 50 years,*)
> R.Watson (N. Brealey Publications, 2008)

It is well worth seeking a personal reputation for integrity. Championing it may prove challenging and even cause some initial unpopularity. Yet, in the longer term, doing so will tend to create a favourable impact. This is liable to be career enhancing not damaging. You may well inspire those around you to act correctly too. To assess your own position do you:

◆ Say what you think?

◆ Risk being wrong?

◆ Avoid actions which harm?

◆ Do what's right even when no one is looking?

1 *Say what you think.* This is one of the foundations of integrity. People want reassurance that you are being true to yourself. Sharing what you think is right and wrong does not mean showing discourtesy or rejecting opposite viewpoints. Instead, you act on the assumption your beliefs are logical and based on fact.

2 *Risk being wrong.* When handling risk, ethics and other choices, you may never be sure you entirely understand the situation. Gather the evidence, attitudes, perceptions and feelings surrounding it. Without complete knowledge you must trust your core instincts and let these guide your behaviour. For example, speculating that someone is inflating sales figures is not enough. Share both your concerns and the evidence.

'The moment of greatest integrity is when we realise we've made a mistake.'

Buckminster Fuller (engineer, systems theorist, author, designer, inventor, and futurist)

3 *Avoid actions which harm.* Google claims 'Don't Be Evil' is a core part of its identity. This is a sound basis for judging choices. But putting all your management behaviour through such a filter can be tricky. A simpler way is to ask: 'would I do this to someone I love?' Even the best intentions may go awry. One firm decided to reward auto mechanics with a high fee for carrying out repairs. This led to repairing things that weren't broken.

4 *Do what's right even though no one is looking.* A famous Olympic golfer once penalised herself two strokes when she accidentally played the wrong ball. Asked 'why did you do it, no one saw you? Nobody would have known', she replied 'I would have known'. Such integrity challenges each of us to check in with our core values.

Sometimes to make your job easier, the occasional lie, or failing to do what is right can seem tempting. Gradually, though, colleagues realise and you risk damaging your credibility. The management challenge is how to fuse high performance with high integrity.

How best can you support the organisation in the struggle to show and maintain integrity? Simply asking relevant questions can be a major contribution. Another is demanding clear, well-communicated ethical rules. Regular monitoring of ethical conduct and remedial action are two further ways of building the right culture.

A matter of character

Changes in laws, regulations, stakeholder expectations and media scrutiny can have catastrophic financial results. Citigroup, JP Morgan Chase, Computer Associates, for example, all faced liabilities running into millions when things went wrong. Anticipating integrity land-mines is challenging, particularly for new and young managers. On the one hand, you face pressure to 'trust your own judgement'. On the other, those at the top expect you to conform and follow compliance requirements.

bringing integrity alive depends less on rules than character

Bringing integrity alive depends less on rules than character. Much of the richness of life comes from sticking to one's beliefs. For example, how important to you is being popular? A desperate hunger to be liked may distort vital choices.

Management is often portrayed as a rational, fact-based discipline. Success, though, will also depend on your ability to value the human dimension. This requires an understanding of the context in which choices occur. Many young managers, for example, resolve ethical dilemmas by using personal preferences and individual values. Yet these need to be within a policy context, otherwise they may prove misleading.

Integrity in action

A commitment to:

◆ Character over personal gain

◆ People over things

◆ Service over power

◆ Discipline over impulse

◆ Mission over convenience

◆ The long view over the immediate

Source: John Maxwell, *The 21 Irrefutable Laws of Leadership,* 2nd Revised edition, Thomas Nelson, 1 Oct 2007.

Integrity drivers

What drives integrity in your own organisation? Can you detect the forces pushing you and others to act correctly? For instance, do formal compliance requirements mainly translate into a box-ticking mentality? Are basic commercial pressures forcing attention on the issue? In some companies customers help drive corporate correctness. They expect it to 'do the right thing', explains the UK managing director of Mars. Many others find being ethical pays because it:

◆ Enhances the brand or reputation

◆ Improves efficiency

◆ Attracts staff

◆ Conserves and sustains resources

◆ Mitigates business risk.

In its US survey KPMG looked at where employees said they felt motivated and empowered to do the right thing. The proportion doubled in companies with comprehensive ethics and compliance programmes.

Integrity touches on a person's character. By raising the issue you may be regarded as attacking or challenging someone at a deeply personal level. The temptation is to downplay or ignore ethical issues, because nobody dares raise them. A less provocative way is posing a series of questions set in a wider organisational context. For example: 'How do we treat those who disagree with us?' 'Is our decision making sufficiently transparent?' 'Does our culture demand high levels of integrity?'

Responses to major ethical scandals such as the *News of the World* saga are part of a bigger change picture. In 2007 McKinsey found society had higher expectations of companies today and tomorrow than in the previous five years.

Integrity metrics

◆ Set appropriate goals

◆ Have good controls for checking and auditing

◆ Build high ethical standards into all processes

◆ Tackle integrity crises with transparency and urgency

◆ Build integrity into all decisions

Most Important Thing a Company Can Do to Be Seen as Socially Responsible
Unprompted, Total mentions, Trends: 2005–2010

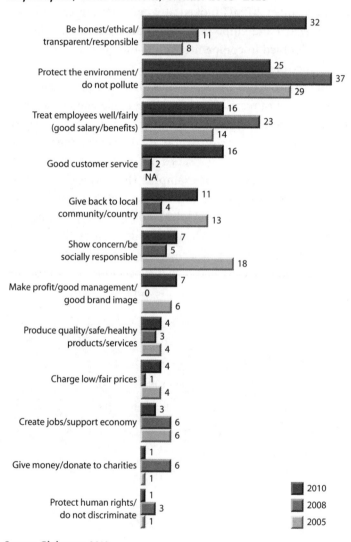

Source: Globescan 2010.

To convert integrity into real day-to-day behaviour is critical to this essential aspect of management success. Ultimately integrity cannot be achieved by a focus on profit, compliance rules, checklists or monitoring systems. It concerns character, courage and a belief in one's own values as much as those of your organisation.

Ways to show integrity

☐ *Treat integrity as multi-faceted, with many aspects you may need to consider*

☐ *Keep a look-out for what is right and wrong*

☐ *Act on your concerns about integrity, even at personal cost*

☐ *Explain when you are acting on your understanding of right and wrong*

☐ *Be willing to speak up on matters of integrity*

☐ *Put potential decisions through the filter of avoiding harm to others*

☐ *Do what's right even though nobody is looking*

☐ *Ask questions about integrity issues*

☐ *Push for clear rules on integrity in the organisation and ensure they are well communicated*

☐ *When raising integrity issues put them in a proper organisational context, such as current policies*

☐ *Become committed to people over things, service over power, discipline over impulse, mission over convenience and the long view over the immediate*

☐ *Assess the drivers pushing your organisation towards ethical behaviour*

☐ *A good way to raise integrity issues is to pose questions such as: 'how do we treat those who disagree with us?'*

☐ *Look for ways to establish some integrity metrics. These might include: controls for auditing behaviour, building high ethical standards into processes, tackling integrity crises with transparency and urgency*

20

Encourage diversity

ALL MANAGERS HAVE A VESTED interest in workplace diversity. Too often, though, it's seen as a problem to be solved – for example, complying with employment law or avoiding discriminatory practices. In fact, diversity creates important benefits (see box below) cutting across many of the issues already covered in *The Essentials of Management*.

The case for diversity is now widely accepted. Most large multinational companies rely on multi-ethnic, multi-cultural teams. Those in Silicon Valley are particularly culturally diverse. This may partly explain why the place continues to thrive and weather the economic downturn.

Most *Fortune 100* firms not only encourage diversity, they like to advertise their commitment in subtle ways: images on their Web pages, diversity in their top leadership, culturally diverse people as company spokespeople, survey reports on their cultural diversity, as well as prominently proclaiming the company an equal opportunity employer. However, organisations are ultimately judged by their actions and not their words or the values they proclaim.

Inject common sense

As a manager you cannot create a diversity-friendly work environment entirely by yourself. But you can take initiatives, without waiting to be pushed. For example, you can choose to inject a healthy dose of clarity about the organisation's sense of what behaviours, values and attitudes it expects from managers and leaders. Let people experience you talking about the importance of diversity and encouraging it – and, most important of all, living it. This will enhance how people view your effectiveness as a manager, within the broader context of the organisation as a whole. Aviva managers, for example, have encouraged the creation of a group focused on sexual orientation which helps to discourage 'gay' jokes.

Do you have the flexible mindset that goes with encouraging diversity? For instance, are you willing to re-think jobs, including how people perform at their best? Secondly, you may be surprised at the strength of evidence in favour of diversity. Maybe it's time to do some digging into the benefits of having a diverse workforce.

Why diversity matters

◆ Creates a more motivated workforce

◆ Produces a more inclusive society

◆ Improves employee turnover

◆ Reduces absenteeism

◆ Generates improvement in productivity

◆ A source of better customer service

◆ Can directly and indirectly affect profits

◆ Provides business opportunities

◆ Enhances individual and corporate reputations

◆ Provides a potential competitive advantage

◆ Encourages creativity and innocation

What is diversity?

Diversity is about creating a workplace that recognises, respects and values the differences between individuals. It aims to maximise the full potential of everyone. Diversity is one part of the process, while inclusion is how those differences are brought into the organisation and built upon. Diversity without inclusion is common but not effective.

More specifically, diversity may involve any of these areas of management concern:

Advertising, recruitment & selection, application forms, shortlisting, interview process, retention and progression, pay banding, training and development, organisational culture, equal opportunities, dignity at work and people-friendly policies

As part of injecting common sense into the diversity issue at work, there are plenty of practical actions you can take to promote it within your own sphere of influence. Two of the most important are: seeing that people feel respected for who they are and what they do; and making sure people make the link between diversity and business success. This might mean chasing up metrics and specific actions that promote diversity.

For example, Symantec the software company has a clear set of goals to encourage the representation of women. They include: a) increase the percentage of women in leadership positions to reflect the overall female demographic and management hierarchy; b) increase the percentage of women at the high end of the technical track in engineering; c) increase the number of women in sales; d) increase the number of women across all technical fields, not just software development areas; and e) build a work environment that supports and encourages women in their career aspirations. As well as executive commitment to ensure that goals and metrics are in place, the organisation has created a number of structures to sustain its diversity and inclusion initiative.

With the aim of injecting common sense try asking: 'Do we measure the diversity of our workforce?' and 'Is there a written plan to promote diversity here?' Specific metrics that support diversity include recruitment data, evidence of long-term retention and promotion, gender and ethnic mix, sexual orientation, and transparency about equal pay. Good intentions around diversity are all too common. It is far better to nail down an actual written plan to promote it.

Other practical actions you can take include:

◆ *Help make the business case for diversity.* There are several drivers for implementing diversity policies and practices, including ethical, social justice, regulatory, and economic ones. But in profit-driven concerns the main driver will be the business case for encouraging diversity. Even though the benefits of a diverse workforce are widely known, many organisations have yet to yet build them into their business strategy. Help make the case for diversity by marshalling and sharing the likely gains with more sceptical colleagues.

In market terms, the known gains include: enhanced understanding of new and emerging markets; winning new business; products and services that meet the needs of a diverse customer base; leveraging diversity of suppliers and other partnerships; enhanced reputation and profile amongst clients and other stakeholders.

In workplace terms, the known gains include: access to wider pools of talent; better staff retention – lower recruitment costs; enhanced employer image/reputation; become an employer of choice; better use of diverse or scarce talents.

Of these many benefits, senior leadership will usually be attracted to a key business gain for their organisation. For example, in one leading pharmaceutical company, the business case for diversity rests on the value of creativity and innovation for bringing new medicines to patients. In Fujitsu Services, who design, build and operate IT systems, the business case for diversity links back to the goal of winning new business.

◆ *Oppose stereotypes*. Leave your race-based assumptions at the door and encourage others to do the same. Sharing racial generalisations, for example, only causes emotional damage. For instance, rather than telling a colleague they have defied your expectations, reflect on how you developed the stereotype in the first place. What made you think like that?

◆ *Discourage dubious jokes*. The workplace is no place for making jokes about race, religion, sexuality, disability or even age. All can involve negative cultural stereotypes. It is hard for those on the receiving end to hit back. Mostly they end up silent and hurt. Some people feel free to make jokes about their own situation, including race or cultural background. But often it is a form of defence: 'I'll make fun of me before you can.'

Set an example and discourage jokes at the expense of race, religion or culture, or

set an example and discourage jokes at the expense of race, religion or culture, or sexual orientation

sexual orientation, even when made by someone from that background. This includes racial banter between colleagues from the same situation. This can be off-putting to others. Some people, for example, disapprove of racial humour, no matter the source. Treat telling jokes based on stereotypes as inappropriate behaviour at work.

◆ *Be aware of cultural holidays and traditions.* How knowledge-able are you about the cultural and religious holidays your colleagues observe? If they openly discuss certain customs, consider learning more about them. Discover the origins of the holiday or tradition, when they are celebrated each year and what they signify. Your colleagues will likely be touched that you took time out to learn about the traditions that mean most to them. When you show this kind of interest, the word gets around that you understand, for example, why an employee takes time off to observe a particular custom.

◆ *Be inclusive in decision making.* The best decisions are usually those using a wide range of thinking and ideas. The starting point is not 'it would be nice to include your thinking here' but 'we really need your different perspective on this issue'. Are employees from diverse racial and other backgrounds actively encouraged to give their view of how best to achieve something? Lead the way in encouraging opinions from a diverse group of people, so they can alter for the better how business is done.

While you may have a clear view of what works, a person from a different background will often have a different take on what will work best. This can increase the depth of thinking and creativity in a work setting.

◆ *Avoid referring to someone by race.* It is surprisingly easy to use language that proves hurtful without even realising it – in relation to age, gender, sexual orientation, ethnicity, and so on. If you cannot recall a colleague's name, for example, it is not appropriate to refer to her as 'that Asian lady in sales' or 'that black girl in operations'. If your workplace is predominantly white, think about how you would describe a white colleague whose name you don't know. You might describe what he's wearing or his height and build. 'That Asian lady in sales' becomes 'the tall woman in the red dress'. By taking a few seconds longer to describe someone, you avoid giving the impression that person's race is first on your mind.

◆ *Make sure guidelines stick.* If your organisation has codes of conduct related to timeliness, dress and ethics, act to see they are applied to all employees uniformly. A white employee should not be allowed 'to get away with' behaviours that a black employee could not, and vice versa.

◆ *Avoid hiring discrimination* particularly by recruiting in your own image. Managers tend to hire people like themselves – the clone effect (see Chapter 18: Select and recruit). Often this is unconscious, yet it happens. The result is discrimination or exclusion of groups. Keep returning to the basic question: 'Could this person make a useful contribution to our organisation?' If there is a concern that disability or family status may get in the way of the role, the focus should be on the requirements of the job and the person's ability to meet them.

Think carefully about the job descriptions you use so they do not exclude people. For example, instead of just listing skills you want, give scenarios about how those skills will be used. About how the interaction within the job will happen. People want to know what they are going to do in their everyday job, how the connections with other people will occur and what the end result will be.

> *think carefully about the job descriptions you use so they do not exclude people*

◆ *Build diversity into your own team*. The more diverse your own team, the more benefits you are likely to gain in terms of fresh ideas, innovation and access to unexpected sources of information. However, differences in communication styles, work attitudes, or behaviour can create friction within teams when these differences are not controlled. Allow plenty of time to integrate the team.

◆ *Communicate the importance of diversity*. Use team briefings, newsletters, bulletins and staff gatherings to convey your diversity message. Use one-to-one meetings for all those directly reporting to you. This also allows you respond to those on flexible working, or part-time, and ensure they are fully informed and up-to-date as much as the full-time staff.

◆ *Identify diversity champions*. If you are responsible for a significant number of people, either directly or indirectly, consider recruiting internal diversity champions. They can help you promote the diversity agenda. They can be people at all levels of the organisation, not just other managers.

◆ *Share out training and development fairly*. Managers usually have a big say in who gets the benefits from training and performance reviews. Yet research from the Chartered Institute of Personnel and Development shows that older workers, for example, are at the bottom of the priority list for companies when it comes to this formal performance appraisal or an investment in development. Make sure all those you manage get a fair share of the available resources when it comes to development.

◆ *Hold a diversity workshop*. Consider enrolling your direct reports in a diversity training session. Make sure it is led by a diverse team: man/woman/ethnicity/sexual orientation and perhaps disability. Make it mandatory to attend, not optional. They may grumble about it at first. Afterwards, they are likely to value their diverse group of colleagues in new ways. A well-run workshop will give people a deeper sense of cultural awareness and understanding of why certain people behave the way they do.

Diversity workshops can take many forms and are usually run by specialists in this area. Sometimes the main focus is on awareness of the legislation. Others highlight how to make the business case for diversity. Yet others show the behaviours needed to manage diversity, including helping people to acquire these through practice and greater understanding. Take a close interest in what you expect your diversity workshop should achieve.

However, inclusion training and development should not be a one-off event. Rather it needs to be part of an ongoing strategy that may take many forms – networks, forums, regularly on team agendas, mentoring (see below), integral part of performance management, and refreshers.

◆ *Law aware*. You will not be expected to know all the intricacies of the legislation devoted to preventing discrimination and encouraging diversity, but at least be aware of the territory the law covers. If necessary, seek help to learn how you might be affected by it in daily practice. In the UK, for example, existing laws deal with equal pay, sex discrimination, race relations, employment rights, sexual orientation, age discrimination and so on. Further guidance can be obtained from sources such as an internal HR department, the CIPD, and from these websites: **www.equalityhumanrights.com**; **www.acas.org.uk**; **www.jobcentreplus.gov.uk**.

◆ *Use procurement.* What a company buys can have an important influence in promoting diversity and equality, both inside and outside the organisation. Check whether your organisation can incorporate specific diversity objectives into its contracts. Partner with local suppliers, as this may bring the organisation benefits of better customer relations, improved market knowledge and build a reputation for making a contribution to the community.

Shifting demographics

The ageing population of many countries has important implications for managers. They must be able to help their organisations draw the best from an older, more diverse work-force. For example, having more workers with disabilities, more female workers and more of a cultural mix all imply different ways of working than in the past.

The demographic shift requires a willingness to handle more varied working patterns. It demands a flexible mindset supported by certain managerial competencies such as com-munication, feedback, planning and organisational skills, setting clear performance criteria, coaching, and a willingness to experiment and change, as well as role-modelling.

Flexible working

◆ Physical arrangements such as remote working

◆ Working compressed hours

◆ Working during term-time only

◆ Allowing time off for medical appointments

◆ Travelling outside rush hour

◆ Adopting a four-day week

◆ Varied arrangements to achieve a work–life balance

◆ A strategy for job sharing

◆ Scope for people to have more time for themselves

◆ Career breaks

IBM, for example, showcase 40 different flexible work packages on their intranet. Any of these can be a headache to manage. Yet, they also help produce a more committed workforce with lower staff turnover.

Get a mentor

Given the complexities of pursuing diversity, there can be no magic bullet to fix the issue. It takes time and commitment and a personal one at that. As part of their diversity programmes, several organisations have introduced mentoring schemes. These help managers develop greater insight into the issues experienced by individuals from different backgrounds and levels in the organisation. For example Unilever Global plc has set up a programme called 'Courageous Conversations', which is designed to help promote cultural change.

If your organisation does not have a mentoring scheme, consider looking around for someone who can work with you on the issue of diversity. It could be a senior manager, or merely someone who comes from a different nationality or ethnic background.

Ways to encourage diversity

☐ *Take the initiative around diversity, don't wait to be pushed!*

☐ *Keep talking about the importance of diversity and be seen to encourage it*

☐ *Familiarise yourself with the benefits of diversity – if necessary, do some personal research*

☐ *Get clear in your mind how diversity links to the business case for it*

☐ *Seek out some of the metrics that confirm diversity*

☐ *Discover if there is a company plan to promote diversity*

☐ *Help build the business case for diversity*

☐ *Watch out for and oppose stereotypes in daily activity*

☐ *Discourage dubious jokes about race, religion, sexuality, disability or age*

☐ *Invest time becoming aware of cultural holidays and traditions*

☐ *Make your decision making as inclusive as possible*

☐ *In ordinary conversation at work avoid referring to anyone by their race*

☐ *If there are codes of conduct about timeliness, dress and ethics, ensure they apply to all employees uniformly. These codes also need to be transparent so that people understand the reasoning behind them*

☐ *Watch out for hiring discrimination in recruitment, whether conscious or not*

☐ *Build diversity into your own team and allow plenty of time to integrate the group*

☐ *Use varied channels to explain the relevance of diversity, including one-to-one meetings*

☐ *Identify diversity champions who can promote the diversity agenda*

☐ *Encourage diversity networks and forums that are accountable*

☐ *Share out training and development fairly*

☐ *Hold a diversity workshop for your direct reports and make it mandatory to attend*

☐ *Update yourself on the main legal requirements around diversity and equality*

☐ *Consider finding a mentor to help you work on the diversity issue*

Sources

BELOW ARE SOURCES for various points made throughout the book. They are not necessarily suggested as further reading although readers may want to use them as such. For a comprehensive list of recommended further reading please visit **www.20ways.dpgplc.co.uk**.

Introduction

Collins, Jim (2001) *Good to Great*, Random House
Hamel, Gary (2007) *The Future of Management*, Harvard Business School Press
Leighton, A. (2008) *On Leadership*, Random House

Chapter 1

Freedman, J. and Everett, T. (2008) *The Business Case for Emotional Intelligence*, Six Seconds network
Goleman, Daniel (1996) *Emotional Intelligence*, Bloomsbury
Serrat, Oliver (2009) 'Understanding Emotional Intelligence', *Knowledge Solutions*
Stern, Stefan (2009) 'Managing the Mood', *Financial Times*, 24 March
Takeuchi, H. *et al.* (2008) 'The Contradictions that Drive Toyota's Success', *Harvard Business Review*, June
TalentSmart.com (2009) 'The Business Case for Emotional Intelligence'

Chapter 2

Barwise, P. and Meehan, S. (2008) 'So You Think You're a Good Listener?', *Harvard Business Review*, April

DeVito, J. A. (2005) *Messages: Building Interpersonal Communication Skills*, Pearson Education

Chapter 3

Jones, G. (2008) 'How the Best of the Best Get Better and Better', *Harvard Business Review*, June

Margolis, J. and Stoltz, P. (2010) 'How to Bounce back from Adversity', *Harvard Business Review*, January

Topper, Mark, H. (1981) 'Coping with Managerial Stress', *Air University Review*, July–August

Chapter 4

Elliot, Larry (2011) 'Euro Solidarity Comes at Too High a Price', *The Guardian*, 20 June

Naya, Vineet (2010) 'How I did it', *Harvard Business Review*, June

Tracom Group (2007) *Creating More Effective Managers Through Interpersonal Training*

Chapter 5

Broughton, P. Delves (2011) 'Brave New Networked World', *Financial Times*, 19 July

Cross, R. and Thomas, R. (2011) 'A Smarter Way to Network', *Harvard Business Review*, July

Ibarra, I. and Hunter, M. (2007) 'How Leaders Create and Use Networks', *Harvard Business Review*, January

Smith, D. (2008) 'Proof! Just Six Degrees of Separation between Us', *Observer*, 3 August

Uzzi, B. and Dunlop, S. (2005) 'How to Build Your Network', *Harvard Business Review*, December, reprint R0512B

Chapter 6

Arruda, William (2003) 'Brand: You; How to Build a Personal Brand to Differentiate Yourself and Create Demand for Your Services', *T&D*, Vol. 57, April

Clarke, Dorie (2011) 'Re-inventing Your Personal Brand', *Harvard Business Review*, March

Corkindale, Gill (2008) 'Return of the Personal Brand', *Harvard Business Review Blogs*, 26 February

Gratton, Linda (2011) 'The End of the Middle Manager', *Harvard Business Review*, January–February

Groskop, Viv (2008) 'Brand Me!', *New Statesman*, 11 August

Harris, Wendy (2007) 'Stand Out and Deliver: How to Develop Your Personal Brand', *Black Enterprise*, Vol. 37, July

Jacoway, Kristen 'Using the Web for Work', July newsletter of *Reach*

O'Brien, T. (2007) *The Power of Personal Branding*, Mendham Publishing

Peters, Tom (1997) 'The Brand Called You', *Fastcompany magazine*, 31 August

Purkiss, John and Royston-Lee, David (2009) *Brand You*, Artesian Publishing

Chapter 7

Drucker, P. (2004) 'What Makes an Effective Executive', *Harvard Business Review*, June

Chapter 9

Schrange, Michael (2010) 'Making Your Boss Look Good (Without Becoming a Sycophant)', *Harvard Business Review Blogs*, April

Chapter 10

Brown, D. and Hirsch, W. (2011) 'Fine Intentions', *People Management*, September

Pink, D. (2011) *Drive*, Canongate Books

Chapter 11

Collins, J. (1994) *Built to Last*, Century

[1] Brad Gilbert's comment is from 'Listening leaders focus on coaching', *The Listening Leader's Newsletter*, 2 November 2005, International Listening Leadership Institute

Chapter 12

Kennedy, G. (2008) *Everything is Negotiable*, Random House

Malhotra, D. and Bazerman, M. (2007) 'Investigative Negotiation', *Harvard Business Review*, September

Sebenius, J. (2001) 'Six Habits of Merely Effective Negotiators', *Harvard Business Review*, April

Sun Tzu on *The Art of War*, translated by Lionel Giles, **www.bnpublishing.net**

Chapter 13

Ghosal, S. and Bruch, H. (2004) 'Reclaim Your Job', *Harvard Business Review*, March

Heath, C. and Heath, D. (2008) *Made to Stick*, Arrow Books

Chapter 14

Sirkin, H. *et al.* (2005) 'The Hard Side of Change Management', *Harvard Business Review*, October

Chapter 15

O'Connell, A. (2007) 'Decision Making, Hotter Heads Prevail', *Harvard Business Review*, December

Chapter 17

Broughton, P. Delves (2011) 'How Jobs Made Apple Fit for the Future', *Financial Times*, 30 August

Coutu, D. (2008) 'Creativity Step by Step, A Conversation with Choreographer Twyla Tharp', *Harvard Business Review*, April

Hamel, G. (2007) *The Future of Management*, Random House

Hamel, G. (2008) 'The Why, What and How of Management Innovation', *Harvard Business Review*, February

Lyer, B. and Davenport, T. (2008) 'Reverse engineering Google's Innovation Machine', *Harvard Business Review*, April

Sutton, R. (2001) 'The Weird Rules of Creativity', *Harvard Business Review*, September

Chapter 18

Collins, J. (2001) *Good to Great*, Random House

Chapter 19

Bazerman, M. and Tenbrunsel, A. (2011) 'Understanding Failure, Ethical Breakdowns', *Harvard Business Review*, April

Cohen, Dr William, 'Integrity is not about Profit', 13 July 2009, Lessons From Peter Drucker by Dr. William Cohen, **www.humanresourcesiq.com**

Heinman, B. Jr (2009) 'Avoiding Integrity Land Mines', *Harvard Business Review*, February

Innmon, J. 'Ethics in the Workplace', **www. hrresources.com**

KMPG *Integrity Survey 2008–2009*

Lee, Matthew T. *The Ford Pinto Case and the Development of Auto Safety Regulations, 1893–1978*, Department of Sociology and Criminal Justice, University of Delaware

Maynard Leigh Associates (2009) 'Integrity: Are Your Leaders Up To It?', *Way Head Series*, No. 5, May

Stern, Stefan (2009) 'Resources are Limited and HR Must Raise its Game', *Financial Times*, 17 February

Vittolino, Sal 'Corporate Responsibility Contributes to the Bottom Line and Improves Worker Engagement', CSR Release 050207.pdf at HR.com

Chapter 20

CIPD (2010) *Focus on the Ageing Workforce,* October
Royal Academy of Engineering (2007) *Implementing Diversity Policies: Guiding Principles*

Index

Note: *italics* indicate a table or figure in the text